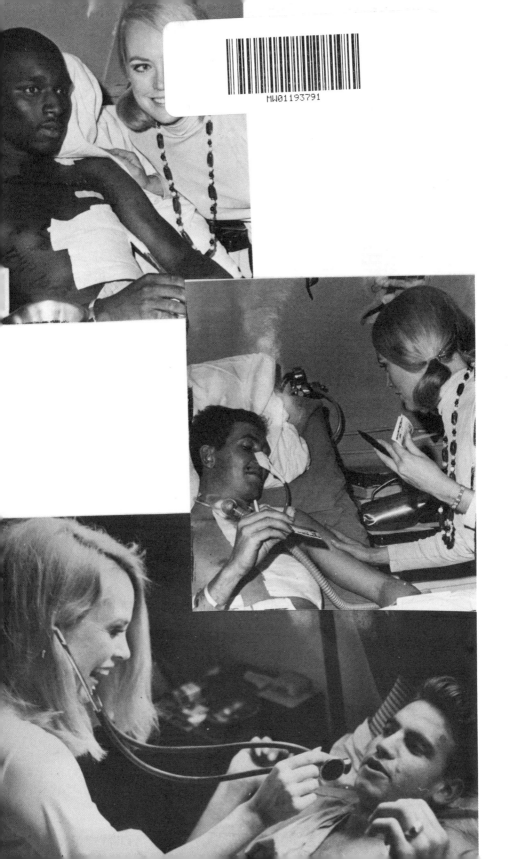

May God bless
you with a
Happy
Life,

Love ya,

Chris Noel

Matter of Survival

The "War" *Jane* Never Saw

by Chris Noel
with Bill Treadwell

ISBN 0-8283-1903-0

Library of Congress Cataloging-in-Publication Data

Noel, Chris
Matter of survival.

Includes index.
1. Noel, Chris.
2. Vietnamese Conflict, 1961-1975— Personal narratives,
American. 3. Entertainers—United States—Biography. I.
Treadwell, Bill. II. Title.
PN2287.N56A3 1986 792'.028'0924 [B] 86-17104
ISBN 0-8283-1903-0

Branden Publishing Company
17 Station Street
PO Box 843
Brookline Village
Boston MA 02147

Appreciation
and Dedication

Two people have inspired me: my mom Helen (Louise) Truax Botz with her love, devotion and presence, and my stepdad, David Henry Botz with his constant and quiet support. I love you for laying the foundation and helping me build my value system.

My sister Trudie Lee Saturno: you have the best sense of humor. I love you, Sis. Johnny too.

The late Bill Treadwell, my talented, loyal friend: this book was possible because of your understanding and encouragement.

Adolph Caso, believing in this manuscript, you picked up the ball and made sense out of my writing. Thank you for your wonderful editing, and teaching me the fine points.

Shad Meshad, my deep gratitude for your kind words: "Chris Christmas, whose goodwill has lighted on so many thousands of men and women during and after the Vietnam experience, may all her suffering and searching for tranquility bring her peace. Her story is still one of the most incredible I've heard ever." My dear friend, here it is in print. You took me on my walk through Vietnam and taught me about regaining strength I never thought I had.

David Yarosh, Marcia Weiss, Don Bush, Rod Burk— my other counselors: you allowed me to talk about things I thought others wouldn't understand.

Jerry Sims and Tom Corey, my veteran friends: Thank you for believing in me. Also, Michael Rhodes and M.G.M. for my start in movies.

To the loves of my life: you are so special and always in my heart.

Trudie Marie, Robbie, Marlo, Gina, Michael and my Godsons Justin and Christian: I have no children. Know that I'm here for you.

Special thanks to my dear friends: Richard Castro, Thomas Girvin, Kathy Kersh, Tom Eggers, Kadyszewski, Dr. Jerry Zupnik, Eileen O'Neill, Rob Atnip, Patty Rautbord Frankel, Christina Campanelli, Lynne Baldwin, Mary Taylor, Jeff, Julie and Tommy Muldavan, Joel and Lynn Johnson, Bill Hancock, Chuck and Angela Greenfield, Mary Scruggs, Victoria Lesser, Tom Sisco, Jim Devney and Peter Spelman, thank you for writing the song that I love to sing, *Matter of Survival*, that inspired a portion of my title, and to those who contributed in some way to this project by way of typing, photo copying, research or encouragement: Carol Gallagher, Frances Wright, Debbie DeLorenzo, Buddy Galon, K-Ann Miller, Richard Fielden, and Peggy Watford.

To David Summers, for hours of copying photos, and last, but definitely not least, to my *Nam* brothers and sisters who served our country well— your life experiences will serve as lessons to many; do not stay alone and keep them all inside you. Share them with others, knowing that you are great Americans.

If it weren't for your sacrifices, there would be little freedom left in the world.

If my words offend, remember God's not through with me yet; if they give a ray of light, then this book will have served its purpose. May God walk with you.

Luv ya,
Chris Noel

Contents

Introduction

"Welcome to Vietnam, Miss Noel. I'm Captain Jim Haas, your escort officer." Many years later, I still remember those words.

Oh my God! Little did I realize this was the first step of a long journey that would take me . . .

Vietnam! What was I, Chris Noel, doing in Vietnam at Christmas time in 1966 instead of being with friends in Hollywood or with my family in Florida?

I volunteered to go to Vietnam because I wanted to do something for my Country. Yes, for my Country!

On one of my Christmas visits with Governor Pat Brown and other Hollywood celebrities at the Balboa and Letterman Veterans Administration hospitals in San Diego and San Francisco, we visited an isolation ward filled with double and triple amputees who had developed gangrene. This was my introduction to the horrors of war.

Jack Jones, my steady boy friend, on returning from Vietnam where he had been part of a Bob Hope show—after many hugs and kisses, said, "I have a surprise for you." He reached into his Jockey shorts and pulled out a beautiful Ruby Princess ring from Thailand.

That night, after a wonderful party, Jack sang songs, then showed slides of his trip with Bob Hope, recounting his experiences with the troops and the people in Vietnam. Immediately, I felt the urge to be part of the war effort.

A member of the National Guard Reserve, Jack spent time with Armed Forces Radio on McCadden Place in Hollywood. One day, curious about seeing a parade of girls, he asked what they were doing. On learning that Armed Forces Radio and Television had not had a woman on-air since W.W.II and that they were looking for a female to do a radio show, he quickly thought of me, and I agreed to try out.

On my audition, my throat was sore and raspy. Nevertheless, a couple of weeks later my dream to reach Vietnam began to come true. I co-hosted a radio show with George Church III called *Small World*.

After only a few weeks, I was called in and told I was fired.

"Fired!" I exclaimed, and here I was giving the show my best effort— it was all a gag. Instead they offered me my own show, *A Date With Chris*.

With the help of producers, Bill Ezell and Bruce Wendell, *A Date With Chris* became an immediate hit with the GIs all over the world. It also took me to Vietnam.

I did not know then that Vietnam would become the dominant force in my life. Its *war* has become part of my psyche, and its effect lifelong.

This story, erratic and rambling as it may seem, is my true story— a story of a person who, today, is trying to cope with the past in order to survive the present. In this effort, I join the thousands of Vietnam veteran brothers and sisters; our struggle in re-directing our lives is a matter of survival, as it should be of concern, understanding and humanity to those who were not directly involved in that war.

1
For Chris (for us all)

Please hear me—
        if my voice sounds distant
        it is because my Spirit
            runs deep
        and affects all that
            I am.
        It is a matter of survival
            (for me).

Please see me—

        do not just recognize me
        look closely and
            beyond
        all that you think you know
            of me.
        It is a matter of survival
            (for me).

Please understand—

        I am your sister
        a child of God
            struggling
        with all that was and all
            to come.

        Within me burns a fire
        that will not cease
            until we reach
        (within and among)
        Understanding and Peace.

        It is a matter of survival.
            (for us all).

2
Am I A Veteran Of Vietnam?

The motion picture and television industry has been good to me. I co-starred with leading men in several successful films and played important parts in television shows. Even though the outer trappings were there, there was something wrong on the inside. Lovely homes and new cars were my way of life.

For more than a decade, since I returned from my last trip to Vietnam, a disturbing and anguishing mental and physical change was taking place in my body and in my mind.

Early on I sought medical and therapeutic attention; but the doctors, who always asked the same questions, never suggested psychological and/or psychiatric help. Instead, they prescribed drugs to counteract migraines, nightmares, numbing in my arms and legs, and other bodily malfunctions. In treating me for allergies and anxiety, I turned into a Valium addict. Not one doctor asked me about Vietnam, nor about my trips there, nor about the dismembered bodies I had seen, nor about how I felt seeing GIs fighting for life.

Finally, in thumbing through *Ms. Magazine*, I came across an article about Shad Meshad and his Vet Center outreach programs, whose counselors became involved in a readjustment program called, "Walking Through Vietnam". Would I also qualify for their therapy?

I was not a veteran in the legal sense of the word. Then I made myself remember something I tried to forget: I am a widow of a Green Beret— the elite of the Army's Special Operations Forces. According to that article, veterans and their families were eligible.

Delayed Stress Reaction

I called and got an appointment with a team leader. While waiting, I picked up a booklet published by the Disabled American Veterans. Nervously, I thumbed through, stopping on the title, *Delayed Stress Reaction*. As I read the symptoms, it was like getting hit over the head. The diagnosis described the same actions and reactions I felt: depression, anger, anxiety, sleep disturbances, psychic and emotional numbing, survivor guilt, and so on. What impressed me was its summary: "the major responses seen among veterans suffering Delayed Stress Reaction to their experiences during and after the Vietnam War have been compiled by psychologists and psychiatrists working with the Vietnam Veteran Outreach Program. Most veterans show only a few of these responses. It should be remembered that Delayed Stress Reaction, also called Post-Traumatic Stress Disorder, among Vietnam veterans, is not a mental illness. It is a reaction to the extreme stress these people were placed under during and after the war in Southeast Asia."

I marked my responses which included negative self-image, problems with intimate relationships, tendencies to fits of rage. The only response I didn't mark was "tendency to react under stress with survival tactics." I associated this with taking a gun and doing something drastic.

Was this what was wrong with me? I had never heard the term, "Delayed Stress Reaction" or "PTSD" or "Post Traumatic Stress Disorder". Was I a victim?

Even though it was hard for me to understand, because Vietnam was long ago, I was convinced I was a victim.

For about eleven years I was in a semi-hypnotic state, with daily emotional and physical numbing, even though I married a second time, ran a cosmetic company, made a film and commercials and attended college.

Nevertheless, I was full of bottled-up anger which made me think about suicide. I hate guns; I hate pain. So I thought of pills as a way out. Whenever I'd think about it, I realized the amount of drugs I would need from different doctors. Moreover, loving life the way I do, kept me from killing myself. Life was and still is precious though at times driving on the freeway, I often considered going off the side of the road— a split second!

How could I have an intimate relationship when I wasn't willing to express what was going on inside of me? My denial mechanism blocked my feelings. I was not able to love because I wasn't willing to feel the pain. Yet, in my days in Hollywood, I loved Steve McQueen, Hugh O'Brian, and Jack Jones.

What was wrong was Delayed Stress Reaction. I never talked about Vietnam; I talked about my first husband, Ty and his suicide, about our difficult marriage, about the time he dragged me across the room by my hair— I can still remember my hair in his hands. I mentioned these things in therapy but not Vietnam. I never once said that going to Vietnam really messed up my life because I didn't think it had, even though I was a Vietnam veteran in the true and physical sense of the word— a civilian Vietnam veteran. Was I just feeling sorry for myself? If so, about what? I don't   like people that feel sorry for themselves.

My appointment at the Vet Center was with Jim Kirk. After sitting down, I immediately started talking— for few questions are asked. I stopped talking when I felt my body tremble and began to cry aloud.

"You are so fortunate you can cry. I have so many men who come in and they can't cry. I'd give anything if I could cry," Jim said to comfort me.

I thought it was bizarre to see this man sitting there listening to me, being supportive and telling me he had never cried. Obviously he had his own thoughts going through his mind: "Not since I was a little boy, have I cried."

I started telling him about one of my recurring nightmares— parades on parades, hospital bed after hospital bed, and cots after cots of amputees.

My First Show

I remember Christmas Day in 1965 when I joined a group of Hollywood celebrities to visit Letterman and Balboa hospitals with Governor Brown Sr., Rowan and Martin, Chu Chu Collins, Eileen O'Neill (my roommate), Sandy Koufax, Ruth Berle (Milton's wife) and Beverly Adams (who later married Vidal Sassoon).

Eileen and I thought we had been invited because we were pretty and because we could entertain. We worked a routine for *Diamonds are a Girl's Best Friend.* I was Marilyn Monroe and Eileen was Jane Russell.

We were taken to the gangrene ward where we were given masks and gowns. Every case was a double or triple amputee. We were told the scrubbing procedure of their open wounds caused excruciating pain.

Here I was a sheltered young girl with many glamorous things in her life— successful modeling, acting with good parts and beautiful homes; now, this contrast!

My childhood dreams never opened my eyes to the distraught and seamy side of life; it never warned me of physical incapabilities. Now I understand why I went into shock. Most of the GIs were smiling as we entered the ward. They tried to survive by laughing and having a few minutes of fun. At that moment I realized the importance of a friendly smile.

I saw these scenes repeated many times. As much as they upset me, I held the tears back. Learning to smile when I didn't feel like it paid off. It was part of my job. Now, after all the years, these scenes come back and smack me right in my psyche— sometimes in the middle of the night, sometimes in the early morning hours.

One particular scene remains a nightmare: young boys—really young boys— with bits and pieces of their bodies blown away. Jim Kirk and I talked about this for about an hour. Before I left he said, "By the way, I lost my leg in Vietnam." He pulled up his pants and showed me he was wearing an artificial limb. I couldn't believe it. Jim noticed I was shocked and apologized. I turned and hugged him.

When I meet women veterans, it's the same thing. We become sisters regardless of the type of life one leads. The fact is, they're still my sisters, as the men are my brothers. I understand the underlying things happening to them.

Jim asked me, "Why do you always have to hug people?"

"Because it's important to me. Hugging makes me feel good. It's my way of saying I care. I've been alone most of my life, carrying things inside me. I would pull back when being hurt. Now I can say, 'Look, let's just talk about this for a minute.' You see, I'm learning."

Date With Chris with Marvin Gaye.

Date With Chris with Nancy Sinatra.

With Bobby Rydell and COL Cranston in Hollywood.

Her favorite escort officers: Ray Smith and Jim Haas.

3
A Soldier of Fortune

Although there were many turning points in my life, 1966 will go down as the year of determination, understanding and love of my Country. I don't say this to wave the flag; it does happen to many of us. Business leaders drop everything when the President calls on them. Military leaders hand-pick their subordinate officers.

As I have said, Jack Jones arranged my interview with Armed Forces Radio. I got the job! I learned that not since World War II had there been a woman heading the shows. During that period Marty Wilkerson was the only woman on AFRTS. She was known as G.I. Jill.

The program format consisted of chatting and playing songs—not the top 40— but Sinatra, jazz and others, for a general audience. Spots were left open to insert Earl Nightingale and spots on American History. I thought some of these spots were boring.

The mail rolled in. The show became more and more popular. Avalanches of mail came in to me and I personally answered every letter. But when the mail became overwhelming, AFRTS hired a service to help me get my responses and photos out. I never saw the returned envelopes that said "deceased".

Christmas 1966 was almost upon us and Bob Hope's annual show was being readied for overseas. On hearing that I was not included, the Pentagon ordered that I go anyway— the only instructions being to take with me a Santa Claus outfit to entertain men some 12,000 miles away.

I went to the 6592nd USAF Dispensary (AFSC) in Los Angeles for vaccinations against Smallpox, Cholera, Tetanus, Plague, Flu, Yellow Fever and Typhoid—the Department of Defense takes no chances, especially with civilians going overseas.

I took my shots all at one time. What a mistake!

First Time In Vietnam

When the plane arrived at Tan Son Nhut, I didn't think anyone would know me as my pictures had not been sent ahead. When a jeep of guys came driving by the entrance of the airport, I got my first surprise. One of them yelled, "Outstanding! Number One! That must be her! That must be Chris Noel. There's Miss Christmas!"

I smiled and waved, thinking this was going to be some experience.

Captain Jim Haas was my escort officer. On the way to the Armed Forces Vietnam Network (AFVN) compound at Hong Thop Tu, we drove through the streets of Saigon taking every scene in, especially the bustling Vietnamese people.

After my introduction to the commanding officer, I was shown around the station and was surprised to find a news room AM and FM Master control, TV film and record library, telescine and kinescope room, three radio production studios, TV Master controls and one large fully equipped TV studio.

A TV studio? I certainly never expected to see TV in Vietnam. TV had made its debut February 7, 1966. I also learned that our Vice President, Hubert Humphrey had recognized the value of TV and placed strong emphasis on bringing Vietnamese programs to the most remote villages as a way to influence the Vietnamese. However, there were few TV sets.

Jim told me that a Blue Eagle aircraft beamed TV signals to the various bases. The GIs called it "Project Jenny". AFVN aired top US programs that had been shown in the states several months earlier.

I spent a few days recording radio shows and appearing as a guest on the GI shows out of Saigon. Then I was asked to do several weather spots wearing different outfits to use on TV throughout the year. Somehow, it didn't make much sense since the weather changes from day to day. But the studio brass said it didn't matter: the GIs would be so busy looking at me they wouldn't pay much attention to the weather.

In Vietnam, American women were called *round-eyes*. Their appearance was quite rare, especially outside of Saigon. With television vans arriving and being installed throughout South Vietnam, I headed out to the field to Vung Chua Mountain in Qui Nhon, Monkey Mountain in Danang, and Camp Enari on Dragon Mountain. A lot of things began to happen to me.

On seeing this blond-haired American woman in the middle of nowhere, a tank driver wandered off the road, almost mowing down a row of rubber trees.

My first helicopter ride was also an experience. The do's and don't's of riding in a chopper didn't take long to learn. I loved sitting near the gunner on the seat close to the open door, looking straight down. It may sound strange, but the wind and noise level became serenity to me.

One afternoon I went up with a general who told me there was enemy activity in the area. Suddenly, a bunch of people started to scurry away on hearing the chopper. They were Viet Cong! VC! The enemy! It was like going up and looking for the prey of the day.

Later, we landed at a fire support base. The guys just stared at me. I went around shaking hands, saying "hi," being all bubbly; but they just stared. I was wearing a pair of fatigues and jungle boots which fit me great and I loved them. But some of the guys looked disappointed because I was not wearing mini-skirts. "Where's your skirt?" one asked. I changed into a mini-skirt, but kept on my comfortable jungle boots. The guys said I looked like Mamie Yokum in *Li'l Abner*. When I replaced them with white boots, they loved them, and that became my outfit: mini-skirts, white boots, sun-tanned panty hose and occasionaly a bush-hat worn by many guys in the boonies. Some GIs gave it to me for a souvenir.

With the mini-skirt, I became a trendsetter for the local girls, who were quick to pick up fashion— cutting their regular skirts midway between their hipbones and knees. *Stars and Stripes* publication ran a series of pictures showing a group of bar-girls in short mini-type skirts and the captions read, "Chris Noel was here."

I was riding in an open jeep in a caravan on Highway 19 that connects Qui Nhon (a small port city) with Pleiku. Suddenly, snipers started shooting at us. It sounded like the cracking of whips. One of the fellows dragged me out of the jeep and threw me in a ditch, piling on top of me, remaining there until the clear signal was given to move on. Though I was scared, I was also angry at the guy for getting me dirty.

I had a lot of people to see that day and didn't want them to see me this way. I should have thanked him, but I didn't. At other times, when we saw action, I felt like a potato sack getting tossed around, on and off helicopters, in and out of jeeps. Other times I was bewildered, not knowing what was going on and not realizing that nobody else did, either.

There was little privacy for me. I lived in my working clothes, and slept in camps or trailers, or wherever they found a place for me. In one camp, I was put up for the night in a corner of a barracks occupied by several guys. A blanket was strung up to give me some privacy. They warned me to tuck my mosquito netting in and around the bed in case of bugs and rats. During the night I had to go to the bathroom. But because no one had told me where it was, and because I was too tired to think about it, I decided to take things in my own hands. I could hear the tossing, turning and sounds of men in their sleep. Shaking out my boots, I stepped into them and walked over to an old-fashioned type washbasin given to me earlier with a pitcher of water and a towel for my morning wash-up. I could see a shadow of someone outside and was hoping the noise wouldn't awaken the others.

When a chorus of guys began coughing and snoring, I covered the basin with a towel, settled back in bed and waited to dump the urine. I felt so embarrassed. Many times I wouldn't drink liquids before going to bed.

Another time sleeping alone in a trailer, not knowing where I was, only that it was the morning after the 24-hour Christmas cease fire, mortars shook me out of my cot. Since I didn't know the difference between incoming and outgoing, I was scared. Alone and bewildered, with everything shaking, I lay on the floor, then dressed quickly and ran outside in search of my GI friends.

During Tet celebration (the Vietnamese New Year), a bullet entered the AFVN studio, piercing the ceiling and two pages of news copy, embedding itself in the newsman's typewriter.

Somewhere out in the field, on the way to a show, we came under gun fire. As I was rehearsing a song in my head, I didn't pay much attention to what was happening. My escort officer began to yell: "Get down. You stand out and make an easy target in that white blouse. We are under attack!"

I don't think many women traveled throughout Vietnam the way I did or as often. It was purely "ad lib" in and out of LZs (Landing Zones), hospitals and TV studios.

There was little itinerary; no one prepared anything for me. I often felt isolated, alone, just like the field soldiers. Now, I began to understand their problems—leaving home for the first time and facing the problems of war in a foreign land, with little or no knowledge. It wasn't easy.

On another day, we were heading for a firebase— the fifth one that day. As the chopper touched the ground and I was ready to jump out, a soldier began to yell, "Get her out of here, we've just been hit! We have wounded everywhere!"

Many times, so much death and destruction made me want to cry. Nevertheless, I learned to live one day at a time, and thought a great deal on the indecencies of war. My few weeks went by quickly. Before leaving, though, I knew I would be back, even if it meant the summer when it was hot and miserable, and entertainers were scarce. I volunteered for a second tour. For me Vietnam filled a need, and I knew I'd be back even though there was no pay. I sincerely believed I made a difference.

I got far more out of that trip than I gave. When I saw how much it meant to those guys, just to see and talk to a girl from home, I also realized it was important for the people back "in the world" to know that we should be deeply concerned about our boys. I considered GI morale in a very personal way to be my concern.

Back Home, I'm The Enemy

On the way home I stopped in Korea and Japan, thanks to the Armed Forces Network which sent me a ticket.

In Los Angeles I felt different. I was home but 24 hours when I got invited to a party. After bathing and scrubbing for an hour, I finally felt ready for my first soiree.

At the party, I knew very few people except for those I had met on movie sets, or seen elsewhere in Hollywood. A few turned their backs on me when I walked into the room. One came over. "Oh, you were in Vietnam. What's the weather like over there? What were you doing there? You're stupid. Why did you go? You're just being used by the government."

After they drank their booze and puffed on grass, they turned to me.

"Did you have fun? How many guys did you f . . . ? Oh, you're a hawk; you must like war!" they'd say, looking me up and down like I was dirt, and then walked away.

At a similar party, I was accused of being involved with the CIA. I certainly don't see anything wrong with the CIA. We need these people to handle the many unpleasant attempts intended to destroy our America. However, to this group of people, calling me a CIA agent was the nastiest thing they could think of to discredit me. The accusations kept getting worse— penetrating and destructive. Feeling brainwashed, I stopped going to parties.

My concern, however, was to find out what type of music the guys wanted back in Vietnam. Even here, I ran into trouble. The Defense Department did not want tunes about drugs to be played. For instance, I couldn't play, *Puff the Magic Dragon;* however, in Vietnam, one could buy perfectly rolled marijuana in Marlboro packs from eight year old kids.

Ray Charles

I taped several interviews with many celebrity singers. My first was with Ray Charles.

Bruce Wendell and I drove to his Hollywood studio. A staffer took me to Ray's office.

He opened the door to a dark room. "Let me turn the light on for you. Ray doesn't need it," he said.

Mr. Charles was sitting at his big desk. I was nervous about the kinds of questions to ask because now I was asking the questions.

Ray stood up, greeted me and, though blind, walked unassisted with me to his studio and recorded a terrific interview.

Nancy Sinatra

I also interviewed Nancy Sinatra, who turned out to be unusually friendly and nice. She liked my telling her about the GIs enjoying her songs, especially, *These Boots Are Made For Walking.* And I got a kick out of learning that she was receiving combat boots from many GIs.

A Date With Chris

Here is a typical tape I did for a one hour show on Armed Forces Radio which includes recognition of mail from the guys, song dedications and public service announcements. The songs were programmed the day before I did the show:

Hi Luv . . . Welcome everybody to another Date with Chris . . . I'm Chris Noel with all kinds of good sounds for you. This program is brought to you by Armed Forces Radio.

I have a letter from a very special person SP-4 who's with Charley Battery 6/15 Artillery. He writes: "I have a question for you, Chris. How short are the dresses in the States now? The shorter the better."

Well, I have good news for you. They are still short. The mini-skirt is still in. The hemline is about 12 inches above the knee cap. That's right. All of us girls are running around in our mini-skirts. He also asked that I play a song for a groovy group of guys . . . Ernie, Chucky Poo, Harvey, Tom Tom, Skee, Rag Man, Tomato . . . sounds like a wild group. To open our program, here's a Dionne Warwick song for you guys . . . high on the charts . . . "This Girl's In Love With You".

And now back to the mail . . . I received a nice letter from Stephen Brown aboard the USS Redford. He wrote to me . . . yes, it seems he had a problem . . . "Everyone knows how crowded it is on a destroyer. But we have a blank space on one bulkhead. It's just a shade over a foot square, right next to a spare receiver we use to tune in for our date." Steve wants me to send them a picture to hang up there. It's already on the way . . . autographed to you and the guys on the USS Redford. And here's a tune for all of you . . . by the Beatles . . . "Come Together".

And now a special message from Chris to all my friends in Vietnam. Fellas . . . don't get hooked on drugs . . . don't go home a drug casualty . . . If you are having a problem, discuss it with a medical officer or better yet, your chaplain. You're all big boys now, so be careful.

And for you guys who are headed home, don't bring any toys with you or souvenirs that you might be sorry about later . . . like a grenade or any other dangerous ammo and weapons. Enough said . . . (I felt ridiculous doing spots similar to these.)

And now back to our program. This is Chris Noel on a Date With Chris . . . I have a letter from PFC Vell with Headquarters Batt. 3rd Batt. 11th Marines . . . 1st Marine Division . . . He thanks me for the good music and asked

me to play a song for all his Buddies . . . Here it is fellas . . .
"The Letter" by the Box Tops.
Just to acknowledge a few quick notes . . .
Thanks to Spec. 4 Barrows, HG. 4th Batt. 9th Inf. 25 Inf
Div. Coming up, I have a Marvin Gaye song for you.
Sgt. Oaks . . . likes our program . . . never misses any
. . .
Pfc Rice with 4th Inf. Div. Happy Birthday . . . and The
Cats from the 1st Inf. Division— (The Big Red One). Here's
a record, high in the charts, for you fellas and all your
buddies. "Groovin' On A Sunday Afternoon" by the
Young Rascals. That song is also for Charles Pace with the
519th M.I. who writes: "It's monsoon season and it's raining so hard it's like living in a shower bath. The mosquitos
are as big as Hueys."
Another reminder: For you guys living around Saigon
. . . The Mayor of Saigon has asked that you stop drying
your laundry and fatigues on the porch railings . . . REAL-
LY NOW. In a few seconds, that song by Marvin Gaye.
One more announcement, especially for you guys in the
colder part of the world: There's a gas that's an invisible
killer . . . Carbon Monoxide . . . Be sure to take precau-
tions in your car or truck . . . to have your car or truck
ventilated . . . no matter how cold it is . . . you can't see it
. . . you can't smell it . . . you can't taste it . . . Take cau-
tion fellas . . . I want you around for a long time. And here
it is . . . *I Heard It Through The Grapevine* by Marvin Gaye.
7th, Communications Batt., Battalion Supply. He's stationed in Danang. He asked me to play a song for his buddy
from his hometown, Kane, Penn. . . He tells me his Buddy
is out in the bush and he is in Danang. The Buddy is fellow
Marine Rod Ficus, K company, 3rd of the 7th . . . 60th
Mortars of the 1st Marine Div . . . I was impressed because
he wants the dedication for a friend who is working hard in
the bush . . . Anyway fellas, the song is for both of you . . .
Here is one of the real groovy TOP tunes of the day . . .
"Downtown" by Petula Clark.
And now, we come to the mid-point in our Armed
Forces Radio show, A Date With Chris . . . This is Chris
Noel playing the songs you requested . . . songs from the

Top-40 list in the States . . . songs your girl friends, wives and families are listening to, day after day . . .

To answer a few personal questions from you guys . . . Many want to know my hometown . . . It's West Palm Beach, Florida . . . but I have been living in Beverly Hills for a few years while working in motion pictures . . .

A lot of mail comes from you "Screaming Eagles". Other guys write as a group, too . . . Today, I heard from the 5th Transportation Company . . . PFC Milton from Raleigh, N.C . . . . Sp4 Jim from Orlando, Florida . . . Sp4 Bob from California . . . and Sp4 Gene of Mansfield, Ohio . . . They claim they never miss a show . . . Thanks fellas . . .

Here's a song for you all . . . now my Southern accent is coming out . . . Now we'll spin . . . another one by the leading ladies on the charts . . . Diana Ross and The Supremes, singing *Stop In The Name Of Love.*

There are a bunch of guys with the 9th Inf. 25th Inf. Div. who call me Mother Chris . . . I guess it's because of some of the spots . . . the Public Service announcements, during and at the end of the show . . . Don't do this . . . Don't do that . . . Watch out for this . . . Be on your guard . . . They even sign their letters with a big, THANKS MOM . . . Fellas, I don't know how to take it . . . but coming from you guys it's a compliment . . .

So now . . . for all my SONS in this Division, here's a special tune for you . . . By The Beach Boys, *Good Vibrations.*

I like to receive your letters, whether you want me to play a special song for you or not . . . I read all the mail . . . it's getting pretty heavy . . .

Most of you requested pictures of me in a mini-skirt . . . I autographed all of them and a mailing service is sending them to you . . . If you have requested a picture, it should be reaching you in the next few weeks . . . I'm not forgetting the troops stationed in Korea, Europe and the rest of the Free World.

Here's one more song . . . not from Mother Chris but from Chris Noel, the girl with the "Christmas-sey" name . . . A Date With Chris . . . And I have you down on my date book for another musical meeting tomorrow at the same time. So, don't stand me up, okay? Here's Miss Christmas signing off with a kiss from Chris . . . Kiss-Kiss! Bye luv! This is the United States Armed Forces Radio And Television Service.

My Counterpart

Hanoi Hannah's strategy was to ridicule America and our fighting men. A typical quote was, "The 173rd Airborne Long Range Recon Patrol are butchers and cannibals and come from the Institute of the Criminally Insane." Most of our men laughed it off and accepted broadcasts by Hanoi Hannah as comedy relief.

No Comic Relief Here

" . . . the war in Vietnam is going well and will succeed." Secretary Robert MacNamara, 1963.

" . . . the war in Vietnam is turning an important corner—government forces clearly have the initiative in most areas of the country." Secretary Dean Rusk, 1963.

" . . . the war in Vietnam is on the right track." Ambassador Henry Cabot Lodge, 1964.

" . . . If we can get the Viet-Cong to stand up and fight we will blast him." General William Westmoreland, 1965.

4
The New GI Jill?

*H*aving no political leanings— just an actress loving her work, I fulfilled the role of sister, mother and girlfriend for our serviceman— perhaps more girlfriend and sister than mother. When a GI would get a *Dear John* letter and I would see him sitting, looking brave, believe me, I felt like all three.

Although a few women put me down about traveling around Vietnam in a mini-skirt, I was a trendsetter with the mini-skirt. At times I put on fatigues. But, when it really came down to it, the men wanted to see femininity. Feeling *feminine,* I had nothing to hide. So I wore a mini-skirt. As my relations were those of a brother-sister, I didn't feel anybody coming on to me. I was their friend.

My concern was not so much what I wore, or the amount of attention I was getting. I wanted people to know who I was and what my needs were. I wanted them to see further than my face, body and legs, to know Chris Noel as a real person and not just a disembodied radio voice.

In show business, I never had to relate to people as I did in the field where loneliness, fear, anxiety, and boredom were felt with deep intensity. When I was the Rheingold girl, I got lots of fan letters; but none of them had the kind of intensity, the feeling and the desperate reality of GI letters. That desperate reality was an incredible shock, because I now realized that I had a lot of responsibility on my shoulders.

Except for a few times, wherever I went, I was treated with total respect. "What the f . . . are you doing here?" was not that uncommon. But I understood. Furthermore, I really knew what I was doing there, and I shared the feeling of the GI who had just seen his friend get blown up. To him I represented the society that had sent them to Vietnam. Yes, there were individuals with a chip on their shoulders who angrily cursed me. Luckily, they were very few.

Believe me, I went everywhere. My escort officer, a different one on each trip, would pick me up and we'd fly by chopper to the most remote places held by Green Berets—small teams, as small as two guys, with whom I'd spend a few minutes, then off elsewhere in the boonies with other groups of men. In the jungle, guys came out from the grass and from the trees. What a life! So, I understand the occasionally unkind remark. I could sense them thinking: "I'll do my best to keep my sanity for one year."

There was a feeling of abandonment, frustration and doom. It made us question the morality of the war, but not just one side of that war. Most people forget there was another side which, when it comes to the issue of morality, enslavement of untold numbers of people was the order of the day. As for humanity, I didn't see much of it on the Viet Cong side.

"I have one year to serve and won't be able to see my wife or girlfriend. I'll live in this stone-age culture, hopefully I'll survive and get back to my civilization no matter how flawed it may be." Yes, this was the prevalent thought among those in the boonies.

For a few minutes when I was with them, I was able to give them at least some temporary comfort. I realized that comfort was one of the main things men in battle need. I was their sister or their girlfriend, or their sexual fantasy. Yes, I was a sexual fantasy to many, as can be attested to by the many letters I received. Those letters embarrassed me then; but, I'm not embarrassed anymore. As I look back, I say to myself, "Hey, if I gave somebody a sexual fantasy and it gave him some pleasure, why not?" In that larger sense, I guess I was a lot of guys' sexual fantasy. Some nineteen-year-olds had not yet had a girlfriend. Though I was aware of it, I was too busy to sit around and think about it. When I think of the role I was playing, the sexual image was only a small part of it. I learned a lot about being a comforter.

Unfortunately, I saw very few American women in Vietnam. There are many things that women do better than men. For instance, a woman can walk into a room and, with a simple smile, change the atmosphere in seconds. It happened many times in hospitals; faces changed when I showed up. I can see it still. Underneath their breath, and bewildered, they would start with, "What the hell is this? Who's that? What is she doing here?" to: "Wow, look at that! I'm dead and in Heaven. I just died? An angel? A *round-eye!* Am I alive? It's a woman! HOME!"

Yes, these are some of the things I brought to Vietnam—things most women do better than men. So, where were all the women? I realize it would be devastating to the men to see our women having parts of their bodies shot off or to process them in body bags. The nurses all too often witnessed this with our men.

The unshaven, weary faces of our GIs would differ, but not their expressions. I could tell a man in the field and one doing administrative work behind the lines. In the boonies, I saw looks of survival and determination; in Saigon, Cam Rahn Bay and in other more secure places, I saw looks of boredom. In Korea, I saw boredom, men sitting around, just letting time go by; in Vietnam, I saw men concerned on how to survive. The faces were the same, their expressions unforgettable. Too many were in a daze.

Throughout, I had an incredible sense of calm. It was as though, maybe in another lifetime, I had already been through it all which may explain why I was able to remain strong in so many circumstances. I was some kind of little rock pillar walking around doing my job. As an emotional person, I cried very little. That doesn't make me strong; but some inner thing kept me from breaking down. Often I had to say, "Now, don't be emotional about this."

I had to remain detached. It was the only way. Now there are times I wish I could remain as detached as I was in Vietnam. It's that whole thing of the mother finding the strength to lift the car off her kid when she's got to do it. Those who have had these experiences will understand. Mine were catalogued, filed and suppressed for another day in time.

I enjoyed landing on the attack aircraft carrier USS Ticonderoga off the coast of Vietnam. The crew was celebrating the 24th birthday of her commissioning and I was surviving food poisoning from the night before. Between cutting the enormous birthday cake and singing on the flight deck, I threw up in the bowl carried by the officer in white who was kind enough to follow me around. Regardless, the men aboard made me an honorary Tico-Tigress of the huge carrier. They probably thought I was just seasick.

When I went to Vietnam the first time, I said, "Do you mean I'm really going to Vietnam? What am I going to do?" With a little white case filled with 45 RPM records, I took a small portable record player. I would put records on and stand and talk to the guys. I'd dance with them, answer their questions and sign autographs.

I knew I had to have more to offer them than just playing records. So, I went to my friend, Bob Ecton, who helped me learn several songs which I then began to sing.

I may have been confused about the war, but never about my role in or out of Vietnam. When *Time* and *Newsweek* interviewed me, I maintained a neutral stance. "Look, I'm not here to discuss politics; I'm here to build morale. That's what I'm doing." The interviews were hard because they wanted to do political stories. "I'm here combating Hanoi Hannah. I'm the green-eyed blonde who gets on the radio with her sexy 'Hi Luv' and talks to our troops. Hanoi Hannah? I don't give a damn about her. I care for our GIs."

Of course, I also knew about Saigon Sally, the Vietnamese woman who traveled around the Saigon area broadcasting on portable transmitters. Her morale deflating show ended while she was on the air. The last sounds were a crash, gunfire, and a man's voice, "You have just heard the concluding saga of Saigon Sally." I knew this could also happen to me.

Being driven around— Captain Haas in the back seat.

Walking with the GIs.

With Brigadier General Frank Davis.

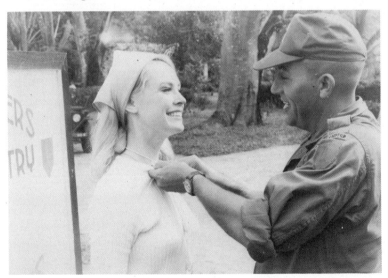

Being pinned by General DePuy, First Infantry Division.

Dancing with a GI.

Entertaining the GIs.

At Duc Pho, with HHC, 11th Infantry Brigade.

Chris between two generals.

5
Acting Career

Why was I performing to begin with? Why did I choose acting as a profession? Feeling shy, I was polite and nice to everyone I met. Liking people, I also wanted them to like me. When I was a little girl I wanted to be an actress. I kept movie magazines and scrapbooks hidden under my bed, because my friends would tease me about them. I loved Marilyn Monroe and always wanted to be like her. Fortunately, I did have some of her measurements. I loved those little Dixie Cups whose tops featured pictures of movie stars, and I loved the art world.

I grew up in West Palm Beach, Florida, as Sandee Noel, a pretty five foot five and a half blonde. I loved baton twirling and practiced it everyday. I wore glasses early in my teens and was bowlegged with buck teeth. In the eighth grade, we had a sewing class with a modeling instructor. When I went home, I said, "Oh, I've just got to be in her class. I want to be a model more than anything."

Unbeknown to me, there were a lot of kids in my school who later became famous. Among them were George Hamilton, Sean Flynn and Burt Reynolds.

At seventeen, I opened my own modeling school, working out of the Palm Beach Ballet Studio in Lake Park, Florida and began to enter beauty contests— I had already won a blue ribbon in the pretty baby contest when six months. A New York photographer came to Palm Beach to shoot layouts. Having been picked as a Kodak girl, I appeared in their print commercials, and then on the cover of *Good Housekeeping* magazine as a young mother holding a baby. I had a drive to do something special with my life. The search was on!

My Mentor

A successful Fleischmann businessman, Frank Hale came to Palm Beach to establish a theater-school for young aspirants—the Royal Poinciana Playhouse, now a landmark in Palm Beach. As one of those aspirants, I had the opportunity to meet Mr. Hale, who, thinking I had talent, immediately gave me a scholarship. Occasionally, he would also give me a hundred dollar bill. I couldn't understand why until he tried unsuccessfully to seduce me. He would say, "Keep it and buy something for your mother." Nevertheless, I continued to go to classes and learned a lot about the theater and about acting.

On my 18th birthday, I went to New York where I had a hard time booking commercials and modeling jobs. I stopped at the Ford Agency and spoke with Eileen Ford, who sent me to the Foster Ferguson Agency where my name was quickly changed to Liz Barrett. But because I wanted to keep my family name, we decided on Chris Noel. I was paid $10 a game as one of the first and last professional cheerleader for the New York Giants Football team. While going from one conference to another, and from one agency to another, I got an offer to do the centerfold for *Playboy* for $5000, which I refused, for the obvious reasons. Turning down that money wasn't easy. As a matter of fact, I had run out of money and had to borrow $200 from my agency in order to pay my bills. Then all of a sudden I became real hot: I was a finalist for the Rheingold Girl,— the most coveted award for models. It offered money, beautiful clothes, limousines, glamour and a lot of media exposure. As soon as I saved enough money, I went to California to see what Hollywood was like.

Elvis Presley

In junior high I first met Elvis Presley— Elvis who? There were several young good-looking girls watching this pimply-faced guy on the stage. Though I thought he was really good, I couldn't understand why the girls were fainting over him. I was fascinated to see so many teenage girls screaming, yelling and crying. When he finished his act, we went back stage to see him, the girls all excitedly lining up to meet him. This very beautiful blonde girl by the name of Elaine walked right up to him and demanded a kiss. After a simple, "Okay honey," Elvis took her into his arms and both kissed passionately. I was standing right in back of her freaking out, to think they were kissing like that. I was so embarrassed. When finally they stopped, and it was my turn to greet him, I shyly said, "Could I have your autograph?" Staring, he took my paper and pen and signed it. Wouldn't you know, someone stole it out of my wallet.

Although later I made a movie with him, for some unknown reason, I just couldn't get it together with him. One day, I was sitting on a stool watching a scene being shot, when all of a sudden I felt a wet tongue in my ear. "Lay off!" I lashed out. On seeing Elvis, I turned red. I didn't know what to do!

"What did you say?" he asked, his feelings hurt. "If that's how you feel about it, okay," he added in an angry tone.

He had parties and invited all kinds of girls except me. But one day, he started to sing "Leon, Leon" (Noel spelled backward) and I knew that things were good between us. Sometime later, a close friend of his told me that Elvis actually liked me. And yes, Elvis even sent me flowers.

One day on the set, while waiting for a lighting change, I asked him, "Elvis, what was it like for you, being a big star, to go into the Army with basic training and all that, and risking your career? How did you do it?"

"I did everything the best I could to the ultimate," he answered. "Polishing my boots or brass, I made certain I did my best. I'm proud to've served my country."

When he died, I thought, "What a way to die!" He left a heritage, a following that mourns his death to this day. Now that I have this war experience behind me, I can further appreciate and respect him as a model American soldier.

Steve McQueen

I was called for an audition to play opposite Steve McQueen in *Soldier in the Rain*. *I was so excited! I got the part!*

The best of this experience was Steve McQueen himself. We saw each other off the set and I must confess he was one of my first loves— and a wonderful one at that. Oh how I wish he were alive!

When I met Steve, I told him I loved his movies, and he was impressed. He asked me about my part.

"A nymphomaniac," I answered, not sure what that really meant other than the word seemed impressive.

"Are you gonna prove it tonight?" he asked with a chuckle.

I had a crush on him from the very beginning. One day, I walked past his bungalow. On seeing me, he said, "Hi, Chris." There was a nice tone to his voice. "Come in," he said, a broad smile on his face. Shy but composed, I walked in. On seeing him busy working with this heavy set guy, I politely excused myself and left.

A couple of days later, he called me to his bungalow. No sooner was I in the door that he took me into his arms and began kissing me. I broke the embrace and said, "No! No!"

"But I've been to bed with every one of my leading ladies!"

The problem was that Steve was married and I wouldn't go out with married men. So, I very politely left.

Several days later, he came up and asked to call me. "We've got to talk," he said, very concerned. On getting a positive response from me, his eyes lit up— just like a little kid, but mighty irresistible. He told me that when he was in New York, he lived with two ladies of the evening. For some reason, that piece of information made him all the more interesting and exciting. But aside from talking about his fantasies, he also talked about his life, including the painful parts.

I followed him in the news while he was in Mexico, where he underwent his unorthodox treatments in Plaza Santa Maria Hospital for his rare form of cancer— mesathelioma, which had spread from one lung to his abdomen and neck.

Members of the press said that even while Steve was wasting away, "you could still see the famous McQueen eyes— piercing bright blue". That is exactly how I remember him.

Hollywood presented different experiences for me. While under contract to M.G.M., I worked with Robert Vaughn and Gary Lockwood in *The Lieutenant* series. I found Robert one of the most unemotional people I have ever met. With Gary, on the other hand, we became an *item* for a short time. During this time, I was under contract with M.G.M. and did *Honeymoon Hotel* with Robert Goulet and Robert Morse. People called Goulet "an 8 by 10 glossy" because he seldom passed a mirror without looking in it. During this time, I also made a lot of beach movies, but the most famous was one with Elvis Presley, *Girl Happy*. Hugh O'Brian was very popular during this time, and we went out for several years. The press felt that the two girls most likely to succeed in the movies then were Linda Evans and myself. *TV Guide* did a story on me, "Happiness is a Girl Named Chris" in which the author placed more emphasis on my dating than on my work. At the time I resented it; now, as I think about it, I never really wanted to be a famous actress, but a great personality— a person! Among the many other things that happened to me was my being selected as the "The Girl of the Year" by the Girlwatchers' Society. I did *Joy in the Morning* with Richard Chamberlain, *Glory Stompers* with Dennis Hopper, and *Get Yourself a College Girl*, with Nancy Sinatra, Mary Ann Mobley and Chad Everett, whom I loved because he was so handsome and down-to-earth.

Frank Sinatra

I dated Frank Sinatra at a time when his mind was obviously on Mia Farrow. One evening, he picked me up at my house and drove to an Italian restaurant on the Sunset Strip, for what I thought was going to be an intimate dinner. On the way over, I noticed a car following us. I asked Frank about it. Shrugging his shoulders, he said they were his friends. At the restaurant, the maitre d'hotel took us to a table having several place settings. Just as I looked up to inquire on the large table, these guys came over and joined us. Thinking the entourage was part of Frank's way of doing things, I went along with it, though I was disappointed. During dinner, the guys kept on talking about Mia Farrow and how different she was from other women. Throughout, Frank hardly said anything, and I did likewise.

After dinner, we all went to a nightclub for a drink. After about twenty minutes, at Frank's signal, we all got up and went to another nightclub for another drink. After about an hour, Frank once again signaled to leave. Outside the club, this man stepped out of the darkness and took Frank to one side. After what seemed like a heated discussion, Frank ordered one of his men to give the man what looked like a large sum of money.

At his house, we sat around having another drink. For some reason, Frank began to pace back and forth. He walked over to the sliding glass door, and all of a sudden began to kick it. To everyone's amazement, with a single punch, he broke through the glass. No one said a word. I couldn't have asked for better entertainment!

After about ten minutes, Frank sat next to me on the couch. After kissing me gently on the mouth, he told me he was taking me home.

At my front door, he took my keys, unlocked the door, kissed me again, and said, "See you around kid."

Burt Reynolds

On a trip back home to Florida, I was introduced to Burt Reynolds, who had been asked to be the King of our local Boat Parade sponsored by Palm Beacher Jim Kimberly, the Kleenex heir. Burt was fun, open, gregarious with the guys and crowds. With me, he was frequently sulking and quiet. He wanted to be a star in the worst way but it wasn't happening to him yet. Nevertheless, he invited me to stay in his New York apartment and I accepted. I still remember: it was dark, and he had satin sheets on his king-sized bed, which kept slipping off. He truly was sensuous.

Burt and I dated several times in New York, Florida and California. He was never on time, however. He had a lot of friends who called him *Buddy*, and I too called him by that nickname.

Our last date was on Burt's birthday. I fixed an intimate dinner for him with all the trimmings and a special cake. When he eventually arrived with his stuntman friend, I called my girl friend, Eileen, to join us. Because Burt was into boats as a hobby, I bought him what I thought was a perfect gift: a beautiful scaled-model yacht, which didn't seem to thrill him too much. In any event, we went on with our meal, but Burt became quiet. Apparently, he was disappointed over my preparing an intimate dinner rather than a party. On finishing the meal, he thanked me and walked out with his friend. A few days later, I ran into the same friend who told me that Burt had given him the model yacht and the other presents I had given him. I was crushed. I guess he didn't like my cooking!

He may never ask me to cook for him again, but we share hometown roots and I know he'd be there if I needed him.

6
The Origin Of My Obsessions

I keep asking myself why more women didn't get involved with Vietnam; yet, they were involved in other wars. In general women are caring, and it is strange to see how so many simply abandoned their men and children. For whom and for what! Stateside women just didn't seem to care much about their returning GIs; many were even unfaithful and unloving. I've met too many veterans who told me they did not have a woman to return to.

In the late 60's, there was not one single woman with whom I could sit down and talk to about the war. Most women I met were radicals, totally against the war. They wouldn't even talk to people who had been there. If they did, they treated them with disrespect. "Those who are in Vietnam are dummies; they're stupid." I've heard it so many times. A popular slogan was, "Girls say yes to boys who say no."

Their attitude reinforced my belief in the need to care about those guys who were putting their lives down for our Country. I began to detest those who screamed and yelled, "Stop the war. Hell no, we won't go!" On the other hand, I had tremendous respect for those who fought for our Country. Vietnam or no Vietnam, soldiers were special then as they are now; they will always be special as far as I'm concerned. I feel citizens not willing to serve their Country should not have civil rights. You cannot have it both ways; you cannot be a citizen only when it suits you.

People attempted to put me down, to discourage me from ever going back to Vietnam. I've lost lots of friends over it. I would avoid going to parties to avoid their discussions. Deep down I knew that I was doing something worthwhile while they were watching the war on television, turning it off when they felt like it. I may not have believed in the war but I *did* believe in those guys. I did not want to argue with them.

At parties and premieres, I didn't feel like smiling. I had seen so much stark reality that parties and the good times didn't fit in. Vietnam had become my obsession, and everything around it made that obsession more acute. I couldn't find a relationship because men I dated could not comfortably talk about Vietnam. Nobody wanted to understand me, let alone bother to ask me about my feelings. They only knew that Chris had tripped off to Vietnam again and that she had come back— and that's about it. Even to my acting colleagues, my Vietnam was just another gig. Thank God for my family and close girl friends.

When my radio show became a hit, my film career suffered. For whatever reason, the wholesome-girl-next-door-type was not in demand. At that time films were changing. Several had nude scenes and I would not do them. I turned down roles such as *In Harms Way* because of nudity. I made it clear that I just would not do nudity.

Veterans coming back learned from their experiences that something was wrong. There was no understanding of what they were doing or why; at the same time, they couldn't go against those who were still in the field because they were their brothers. "How could we win a war we weren't allowed to fight?"

One of the hardest things for me to deal with was the Hawk/Dove issue: "Oh, you're a hawk. You've gotta be a hawk. You go to Vietnam." I just did not want to take sides. I supported the GIs!

A lot of times I was confused and would say, "What am I doing? What is this? Am I a hawk? Am I a dove? Why is there no category for where I am?"— perhaps just nowhere, in no man's land, because I didn't fit in either. It's strange to be in the middle, especially during the time when emotions were so high.

Looking back, I see how young I really was, though we think we're so grown up when we're twenty and can have our cigarettes and liquor. Vietnam changed all that.

When in Vietnam, as I said before, I never knew if that day was going to be my last. I got the same mentality the GIs had in combat, always feeling the dangerous threat to life and limb. I can never forget those mortar rounds blowing up around me. I can never turn off my Vietnam experience as one turns off a television program. I'll never forget the eyes of the GIs.

Those eyes!

The helicopter came in about nine o'clock at night, sniper fire coming from all over the place. I backed up into the bunker for support and protection, then made a flying leap for the chopper, which got off in seconds. To think that moments before I was in front of a television camera talking to a group of soldiers.

Another time, a helicopter's hydraulic system malfunctioned, and we went down in a rice paddy next to a village held by the Viet Cong. I knew what was happening the minute I saw the red light go on. And, as weird as it sounds, going down was more exciting than anything. In fact, I was laughing though tears came to my eyes. I am now sure that many men go to their deaths laughing.

Laughing in the face of death makes me unhappy with myself; it must have been a sick moment. Emotions are so unpredictable especially in the face of death.

Off in the distance I saw soldiers running towards us. The gunner desperately tried to remove the gun mounted on the chopper. He sliced open his hand, and the gash started to bleed as the men formed a perimeter around the helicopter and me, as we waited for another helicopter to pick us up. This was one of several similar battle field incidents.

The fear of death was compounded by the fact that the Viet Cong had put a price on my head.

General Westmoreland and Bob Hope had a price on their head of $25,000.00. My *head* was only worth $10,000, dead or alive. In Vietnam, that was a lot of money.

As the war progressed, I was all too often astounded to see so many stoned GIs, some caressing their love beads. I remember those frightened, half-dead faces. I still see them— a lot in fact! I must admit I found it hard to cope with it then.

A GI handed me an Ankh with a peace sign he had made for me. He was no different than most: no American image of gung-ho servicemen, starched fatigues, polished buttons, or men at attention. What appeared on their faces was despair. The more the war progressed, the more despair on their faces, and on mine!

Here's a letter addressed to me:

Dear Miss Noel:

Today, 19th of March, could be the last day for most of us. We are going to make a beach landing in a pretty rough spot in Vietnam. When you receive this letter I'll probably be gone from this crummy world. I just want to say that listening to your beautiful voice on radio gives us Marines a big lift. It's just too bad that most people back home don't give a damn what happens to us or the outcome of this war. They just keep on protesting and criticizing, but give no encouragement or support. They don't know that us Marines are afraid and want to live like others. I'm just an ordinary young Marine, not old enough to drink or vote.

I've always been a great admirer of you, and was hoping and wishing that I would be able to meet you in person some day, but for reasons now, I can't plan that far ahead.

Best wishes,

Kanary

1st Battalion 4th Marines

H&S Co 2S4

It is said that when you receive something you pay for it either with your body or mind or financially or spiritually. I sure as hell paid for it emotionally. It has made me into a fighter, however; it's made me realize what a survivor I am and how important a good happy life is for me. Back home, there were times I didn't know what to do with my life. In trying to numb out the pain, to self-medicate I began to smoke grass and found it was the only way I could get to sleep. Drugs seemed more prevalent in Hollywood than in Vietnam. It was frightening because most all the men I met used some recreational drug.

Most of the GI's kept a short-timer calendar, each knowing the minute he arrived in Vietnam and the date he would catch the "Freedom Bird" back. Many wrote the return date on their helmets; other wrote things like, "Yea, though I walk through the valley of the shadow of death, I will fear no evil, for I am the meanest son-of-a-bitch in the valley."

In *Girl Happy* with Elvis Presley, Shelley Fabares and Mary Ann Mobley. (MGM)

At dinner with Burt Reynolds, c returning from Vietnam.

With Jon Voight at "Green Ribbon" Unity Day in L.A.

With Hugh O'Brian on vacation.

y in the Morning with Richard mberlain.

In *Honeymoon Hotel* with Robert Goulet. (MGM photo)

th Jack Jones at the Fairmont Hotel, n Francisco.

"My best" to Chris from Bob Hope.

7
Show Business In The Boonies

My job was to concentrate on ways to break the reality of a war— no war jokes, just everything "Home Town", from music to wives to girlfriends.

On seeing one guy really depressed, I asked what had happened. "He looks really sad."

"Yeah," a GI answered, "he just got a 'Dear John' letter."

I walked up to him and said, "I understand you just got a 'Dear John' letter".

"Yes," he answered, looking up and holding back tears.

"Look, she's not worth it. Anyone who won't wait for you, just isn't worth it. You might as well find out now, rather than when you go back home."

I still see those young guys in Vietnam, standing there, looking into their despairing faces.

"Oh God, I know exactly how you feel because I feel the same way. Knowing you go back home and finding that nobody even cares is the hardest part."

I was surprised to see how many young men never received letters of any kind.

Some wives said, "Don't come home. I don't want to be married to a crippled man".

I heard many complaints, saw those looks of depression, and met GIs who wouldn't tell their families the extent of their injuries.

Until you see it first hand, you cannot know the extent of pain and agony. So many of these men were fine soldiers.

I went to Vietnam several times. On one of these trips, I recorded the following dialogue, which is typical of so many I did in the field:

C: Dave Vigrass, it's nice to see you.

D: Hello.

C: How you doing?

D: Just fine.

C: I went to school with you, that's really wild. How long have you been here?

D: Eight and a half months . . .

C: Really, then you'll be going home soon, won't you?

D: In about a month.

C: You know what I'd like to do, I'd like to send a tape to your mom and dad. Would it be OK if I did that?

D: Just fine. Outstanding.

C: Outstanding idea? I'll tell you what I need. I need their names and address. Okay, I'll be home in February. Do you want me to call them for you? I'll try to do that.

D: Please do.

C: What's their number?

D: I don't know . . .

C: You can't remember it? I'll find it in the telephone book. Can I?

D: Yes.

C: Do you have a message for them?

D: Merry Christmas, Happy New Year, and I wish I were home.

C: It'll be after that. I'll take it to them when I go home in February. Is there anything else that you want to say to them? What have you been doing since school?

D: Well, I went to supply school for six months, and then I came to MCB 10, and we spent about two months in Port Hueneme in California, and then we deported to Vietnam.

C: Have you ever been to Los Angeles?

D: I was there once, in Pasadena, and I saw my room-
mates' mother-in-law.
C: Oh yes, okay. I'll try to find your Mom and Dad and
give them this tape. Okay Dave . . .

I liked some of the Vietnamese people—their gentleness
and strength, and how nice the women were. As much as I
think Orientals are the kindest; they're also the fiercest. I
saw a lot of beauty there, and so much pain.
    I remember seeing, in a medic's tent in the middle of a
field, a father with such pain in his eyes looking at his little
boy with a huge stomach bulging out, dying in front of us,
with the medic and I helplessly looking on. The child deeply upset me but not as much as the distraught father. I'll
never forget that look of pain in his eyes. I told everybody I
needed to be alone. I went out and cried and cried. It was
the first time I had seen what was happening to children.
From that point, I never quite got this out of my mind—
just like those scenes in the hospitals.
    At a hospital I saw a man with his nose blown off.
Standing there I felt helpless and afraid. "Oh God!" I
thought, "his nose is blown off his face!" I couldn't believe
it. I had seen many arms and legs missing from my brothers, but not this.

Hugh Mulligan, an Associated Press correspondent,
went with me to Lai Khe and other areas. During this trip,
the 1500-man First Infantry Division known as the *Big Red
One*, officially adopted me as one of theirs. Its Commander, Major General E. Depuy, presided over the ceremonies
which were taped on December 26, 1966.
    The following are excerpts taken from tapes made on the
26th December 1966, 1st Infantry Division Headquarters,
at Di An, between General Depuy . . . G, and me . . . C.
    G: Chris, I just want to thank you very much for coming
to the First Division, and my only regret is, that you haven't had the time to go and visit all of our troops, because I
can tell you that they love it. I invite you back right now in
hopes that you'll be able to manage that. We could use you
full time right here. Even though you are only gonna be

here for a very short time, I want to give you this Certificate of Appreciation. We'd like to adopt you in the First Division. And it's not a bad division to be adopted into, I might add . . .

C: Gee, it sure isn't. That's very nice, thank you very much, General, thank you.

G: Chris, please come back.

C: I hope to, in a few months.

G: And we're gonna give you a Big Red One— pin and patch, I'm not sure 'cause you don't have any buttons on your chest. You might be able to find some way to wear it.

C: I'll wear it on my fatigues.

G: Yes, that's a good place to wear it, particularly when you visit other divisions. Will you do that?

C: Oh, I see, alright. Thank you very much; that's very nice . . .

I didn't know what was expected of an adopted daughter. However, I promptly went on my way living up to the famous motto of the Big Red One: "No mission too difficult, No sacrifice too great, Duty first."

An orientation officer was giving a lecture to newly arrived replacements. On walking by, I popped in to welcome them to Nam. When I left I heard the officer laugh and say, "Men, as I was saying about booby traps . . . "

I trooped out to rifle companies where I chatted with the boys in sandbag bunkers, danced on mess hall tables and played Rock 'n Roll on the little portable phonograph. I also visited guys on perimeters, knowing how much it meant to see and talk to a girl from home. I even visited the men of unglamorous motor pools, maintenance shops, graves registration and the morgue.

One time I pulled the lanyard cord on a 105 Howitzer. A GI handed me ear plugs, then asked me to sign the shell, "To Charlie, lots of luck, Chris". It was aimed into an abandoned rubber plantation five miles away. Another told me it was aimed at a suspected VC village. I preferred to believe the former.

Later, my ear plugs were raffled off with the money going into a scholarship fund for children whose fathers had died in Vietnam.

Al Chang, the combat photographer, took lots of photographs, and Hugh Mulligan wrote several articles that appeared on front pages throughout the world.

Days later, the Commander of AFVN— I believe LTC Dee Ballou— scolded me for having pulled the lanyard. It seems a doctor in France was upset about a civilian firing weapons. Knowing what the civilians did on the other side, my pulling the lanyard becomes ludicrous. Nevertheless, the Pentagon agreed with the Frenchman.

I felt it was going to be fired anyway, so it wasn't such a big deal at the time. Now, of course, I realize the importance of those regulations prohibiting civilians from firing those weapons. I only wish it applied to all sides.

Interview with Captain Haas:

C: What things impressed you the most on this trip, Captain Haas?

H: What impressed me most was you, Chris.

C: Oh, forget about that.

H: No, really, that's what impressed me. I've been up country a number of times, so I wasn't impressed particularly by seeing the people and the things, 'cause I've seen that before. This is my first chance to see somebody who really cared about these guys, in the truest, deepest sense of the word. Doing a lot of good for them. This is what really impressed me, and I'm not kidding a bit. You went out there and made so many guys happy, probably the happiest they'll be in their whole year here, except maybe the day they go home. To me it was just really tremendous the way they responded to you, and the way that you responded to them. You instinctively knew what they needed, and you gave it to them.

C: What things happened that you think should be remembered?

H: Well, the things that I remember mostly are the hospital wards, because, first of all, we went into so many of them, and secondly they reacted in such strange ways. It's understandable when a guy is sound asleep, and he wakes up, and he sees something like you looking right down at him. He can't think of anything really, except, "My God, I've died and gone to heaven." I'm sure there were cases where they felt just that way, 'cause I remember one guy who opened his eyes, looked at you, closed his eyes again and started feeling his arms. He couldn't believe that he was still there. This really impressed me; and also, every place you went, the word spread like wildfire, both in front of you, and in back of you. Many times you couldn't see the reactions that I saw because I would stay behind just for the fun of watching them. Sometimes when we would go into the hospital wards the guys would look up at you, and then they'd look back down at what they were doing, putting a puzzle together, or whatever it was that they might have been doing. I was really disappointed sometimes, with the way some of the guys acted, but as you would leave and they would look at you from behind, the whole attitude changed. It was really something to watch. The funniest thing that happened was the way that we practically destroyed the Red Cross building, the recreation lounge up at An Khe. It was just numbers of troops from the whole division, and it was right in the division headquarters itself. They brought buses and truck loads of guys from all over, so I couldn't tell you what group it was.

C: Wasn't it the First Cavalry.?

H: That was the First Cav Division, right. Of course guys were crawling on the rafters, and wherever they could get, so they could get a decent look at you, and the building was just not built to handle that kind of a crowd. It practically collapsed right in front of our eyes.

C: The funny thing was the sign on the building the next day. The sign said, "Closed for repairs." What else happened that was funny which you remember?

H: Well, the old truck that Captain Leach had. It was the only thing that even came near to being a closed vehicle. It was raining all the time there. The only other vehicle that he had was a jeep; and this old truck not only leaked, but it didn't run very well. One day, when we used it all day long, the truck broke down when we were in the Seabees regiment, and the Seabees had to fix it.

C: That was MCB 10, and that's where I saw the fellow that I went to school with— Lt. David Vigrass.

H: Yes. That's also where you saw the Chief of Chaplains in the Navy. To get back to our story, the vehicle finally died as we were on our way up to the television studios on Monkey Mountain to make your hour and a half television show. We scrounged a ride from an R.M.K. guy who just happened to drive by with a pickup truck. R.M.K. is a gigantic construction firm, a combine of construction firms, that are doing the great majority of the building work being done in Vietnam right now. Anyway, it did get up to the top of the hill, and Don Leach got his comeuppance because he had to ride on the back of the truck in the rain, and he got quite soaked by the time we got up there.

C: That was a good show, good entertainers, don't you think?

H: It sure was. I didn't see all of it, but what I saw was real fine. We went to a club at the bottom of the hill, an Air Force type club. They were presenting an award to the Vietnamese Airmen of the Year. This was the place, if you remember, you commented later on where the colonel was so gruff . . . He was ordering you around the stage: "Stand here, take these, stand over there, and get in that picture."

C: Who were those guys up there on the very top of Monkey Mountain? The guys that took care of the missile?

H: That was the First Light Marine Aircraft Battalion, B Company, and they were the guys that were responsible for providing security in the area for their Hoff missiles. I just want to say Chris, that one of the memorable parts of your trip to the 25th Division at Cu Chi was when we were driving to the mess hall, where you were to meet up with Bob Hope, and I was sitting on the outside of the jeep, sharing the front seat with you. We stopped in front of the mess hall, and all of the soldiers were lined up waiting to have lunch with Bob, and they saw you, and I watched all the cameras come up in unison, at the same time, and I knew right away, that I should get out of the picture, and I headed toward them, and just as I passed them they all clicked at the same time, and it reminded me of locusts in a field of corn. All the shutters, and all the clicks! I just thought that you would want to record that as one of the memorable occasions of your trip . . . Chris, this is Bill Sheppard, I'm the information officer of the 25th Infantry Division at Cu Chi. This is the 25th anniversary of the 25th Division.

Bob Hope Special

Bob Hope celebrated his 25th year at entertaining the troops over seas, and did it with the 25th Division on the 25th of December. I still remember his introduction:

"North Vietnam has Hanoi Hannah, and our government decided to do something about it. So they have a gal who's sort of gonna be a counterpart of that and I'm sure she'll top Hanoi Hannah by a long shot, because she's one of our most beautiful gals. She's from Hollywood and I know she's doing a great job, and I want you to meet her this afternoon . . . CHRIS NOEL . . . Miss Christmas, right here! . . . (tremendous screeches and howls from the audience):

C: Hi Luvs.

B: Darlin . . . from this reception I think you're gonna be quite a smash here, and I think you are darlin'.

C: Thank you, Bob.

B: I know you have quite a job here, and I know they picked the right material for this job, and I know you'll be able to work without Johnny Grant, won't you?

C: Johnny's my friend. He also has a show on AFRTS.

B: I tease Johnny every once in a while, well anyway he's around here. How long are you going to stay around here, darling?

C: I'm not sure. I go to Korea and then back to Los Angeles for more recordings.

B: Are you gonna come back, or are you doing just a short stay here?

C: Well, it's up to these fellas if I come back . . . (screams).

B: I think they'll chip in and get the fare, myself . . . I think you're just marvelous, and I'm thrilled to see you. You haven't been on my show for a month or so, have you?

C: No.

B: And I think you're great, 'cause you bring an awful lot with you . . . (laughs).

C: Thank you.

B: Chris Noel, how about that . . . Now Chris has a poem that she wants to read, and I would like to hear it too.

C: Well, this is interesting; it was given to me last night. I think it's appropriate for Christmas, and this is for you guys. Are you ready? (More screams).

'Twas the night before Christmas; things were not so hot,
not a creature was stirring, for fear of being shot,
all the stockings were hung, in the bunker with care,
they'd been worn since we landed, and needed the air.
Throughout the night, there rose such a chatter
that I dashed through the night, to see what was the matter.
Up in the sky, you never saw such a sight,
mortar explosions everywhere; the sky was bright.
Christmas presents from Charlie, landing here and there.
Then suddenly appeared from out of the night,
a strange wild, vehicle, what a beautiful sight
bringing an end to the party, but no one would resent it
for peace on earth, good will to all men,
it's us One and you Ten (as this was before Bo Derek's movie "10" . . . applause and yells from all the men).

C: Just in case you're wondering, this is a mini-skirt, and this is what they wear in the states.

B: I'm glad she said that, cause I thought something had shrunk. May I say that this is not our final number, so don't get up and leave. We have a final number that I think you'll enjoy. Let's bring out the girls. (End of tape)

My Second Trip

Captain Ray Smith, my escort officer on my second trip, spoke French and personally knew many Vietnamese. He introduced me to several of them. Once, he took me to the home of a doctor; there I met his daughter with whom I became acquainted. In contrast with the rather pleasant home of that doctor, I was almost always startled to see little huts with television sets— in the middle of all that poverty, war and destruction.

Captain Smith was just absolutely wonderful. So was Jim Haas. I think about them a lot.

Typical scene in a Mess Hall, December 1966, which I recorded (I spent the first few minutes saying "Hi" to everyone; pictures being taken, a lot of loud laughing among the many men)— *C-Chris; V-Voice:*

C: Hi . . . Hello . . . Hello. Did I miss anyone? Did I get everybody?

V: What's that you've got on?

C: It's a mini-skirt and jungle boots.

V: I thought it was something like *Lil Abner*, you know (much confusion, lots of voices, screaming, laughing).

V: Merry Christmas Chris.

C: Merry Christmas; it's good to see you. Thank you. Where shall I go? (Moved around) Hi, Merry Christmas everyone . . . It's a mini-skirt and jungle boots. You like the skirt huh? Should I sit here?

V: Your name is happy, like a holiday. Would you like some coffee?

C: Do you have anything cooler to drink . . . Thank you. I like that . . . You have some Kool-aid? Cherry Kool-aid? (Howls, laughter, hundreds of people are having a wonderful time). Yeah, I came to Danang yesterday. Well, I have an escort but I don't know where he is. Well, we're leaving here tomorrow morning. We're going somewhere but they won't tell me anything about it.

V: Who's this?

C: The people at Armed Forces Radio said that they want me to go there. Then I'm on to Saigon and I'm not sure where I go after that.

On Christmas day I landed at several fire bases and LZs. I was amused to see *their* Christmas trees: sticks in the ground decorated with empty C-ration cans and GI boots, capped off with steel helmets.

Medical Miracle

An interview about a medical miracle:

C: Dr. James Chandler, you've just had an operation that was really extraordinary. Could you tell me about it?

J: Well, let me start a little bit on the background. This is the third live grenade that's been removed here in Vietnam that I'm aware of. The first one was done by a major with General Humphrey down in Saigon a little over a year ago. Then approximately four months ago, Captain Harry Densmore of the US Navy over at Danang East removed a live ordinance from a human body. This one is different from the others in a couple of respects. One: I don't have that rank; Two: those people both knew what they were dealing with before they went in to do the operation to get it out. I didn't know ahead of time what I had to deal with. This M-79 rifle grenade popped out in my hands as kind of a bad surprise.

C: I bet it was. You took an x-ray but you couldn't tell what it was, could you?

J: It was worse than that Chris. I took the x-ray and could see the metal thing— it was so big. I couldn't believe it was in that man's throat. I thought it must be something that was just laying on the stretcher.

C: Really! Isn't that something? And what did you do when it popped out?

J: Well, when you're in the room, the operation takes place with about nine or ten people helping me so it became obvious that I just couldn't leave it there. I was holding it. There was nobody there to give it to, so I walked it out carefully, and took it out about a hundred yards. Then a Marine came and exploded it for us.

C: Well, that's very interesting. Imagine, a live grenade in a man's neck! How's the fellow doing now?

J: He's doing very well. He's 20 year old Marine Private Raymond Escalera from L. A., and he should be in Clark Hospital now. He stayed here 36 hours following the operation, and he showed at that time an enormous spirit and seemed to feel quite well. I think in the long run it'll take him some time to get all healed up. But he's gonna be fine.

On a trip to Long Binh, I noticed a barber shop named *Chris Noel*. What a thrill! It had a pole in front and signs in the window— Haircuts, Shaves. Excited and honored, I walked in to meet the barber, only to find out it was a front for the local brothel. I was shocked— my name being used for bait! On the Quin Nhon coast, there was another *Chris Noel* Barber Shop. This time I didn't bother to check it out.

Other Women In Vietnam

Red Cross girls usually avoided entertainers, their attitude was, "We're here all the time; let them have their day."

On my first night with Red Cross girls, I was fascinated watching them picking out dresses from a Sears catalog. While chatting with them over their choices, I heard this big noise. When they started running, I yelled, "What is happening?"

"In-coming! In-coming! Get in the bunker!"

The nurses wore 'greens' and were confined to the hospitals, always looking worried. Some resented the "Donut Dollies" wearing their pretty clothes and traveling around freely.

The first Purple Hearts given to women were awarded to: LT. Commander Ruth Ann Mason, LTs. Ann Reynolds, Frances Crumpton and Barbara Wooster. They were Navy nurses wounded on Christmas Eve 1964 by a VC bomb which hit their hotel in Saigon.

Dickey Chapelle, a war correspondent often parachuted into action with the Marines.

On patrol, a trip line booby trap exploded hitting her in the throat. She died on a field of hundreds of punji sticks set by the VC outside Chu Lai on the second day of Operation Black Ferret.

Barbara Robbins, a twenty-year-old stenographer from Denver, was killed by a VC bomb that hit the American Embassy. She died at her desk holding a ball point pen.

A Letter to Santa Claus

"Dear Santa: This Christmas I have decided to ask for only one present. Since there is no snow here in South Vietnam, you can't land, so just wrap it and I'm sure the Postal Department will take care of the delivery.

Santa, can you imagine the joy on my face when I open your gift and find the one thing I want most in the world— an anti-Vietnam demonstrator.

"At least I'd have someone all mine, to share my exciting experiences with.

"I promise I'll take special care of him. I'll give him a haircut (they all seem to need one) but I can't promise to keep him clean, because baths are pretty scarce over here. Besides, dirt seems to be a prerequisite for protesters; he should feel right at home.

"I'll share my bed— and sometimes inedible food with him. I'll share the diseases, the intense heat and the impossible steaming jungle. I'll share the misery of trying to identify their mutilated and tortured bodies that the Cong leave behind.

"I'll let him sit beside me in my waterfilled foxholes—waist deep in mud. And Santa, I'll be warm with the joy of giving this Christmas present you were so thoughtful to send me, a little hell.

"I promise, Santa, to always let him have his own way for as long as he lives; of course that won't be long if he insists on saying the things he said in the States.

"The next time one of our patrols is attacked by the Cong, I'll let him run to the front to tell them he loves them and wants to help them.

"Santa, for the New Year, I have decided to ask for another present. Do you think you could perhaps send all my buddies a demonstrator for their very own?

"I am a resident of Los Angeles, California, when I am not in Vietnam.

"William Holmes Jr. 221 42 PFC
USMC 2nd Battalion, 9th Mar."

Declared or not, the war created anger and hostility, and a divisiveness America had not seen since the Civil War. Ho Chi Minh kept saying to his people, "Stick together" and they did, contributing to their war effort the likes of no other people. They had patience and lived on monthly allotments of eight pounds of rice and one pound of meat. These people knew nothing except struggle.

As I faced each day, one particular thought went through my mind, over and over again, "Ask not what your country can do for you; ask what you can do for you country," said President John F. Kennedy.

Singing *Sonny* to shy and reluctant PFC Roy Hanson.

Singing to SGT Doug Westney in Chu Lai RVN.

On a platform entertaining the troops in the field.

Writing a note on a live round, "To Charlie . . . "

8
Hi Luv!

The Pride Of Armed Forces Radio In Vietnam

Typical dialogue aired on AFRV (V: GI Voice, C : Chris):

V: First Air Cav. welcomes you, and I understand you have some great records lined up for this part of the show.

C: I sure do, but first of all, I'd like to say that I hope this has been a great day for all of you and especially the guys of the First Cav.

V: Well, we're certainly glad to have you; what have you been doing? You arrived last night, isn't that right?

C: Yes. Well, last night I had dinner and went to all the different clubs and said hello to everybody.

V: Okay, how about a song now, Chris?

C: Sure, the first one is *That's Life*, Frank Sinatra's new big one . . . (song is played). Oh yeah, Frank baby, that's life. He's right about that.

V: It's what's happening, life, I'll tell ya . . .

C: That's right.

V: Seems that nine out of ten people like life.

C: Well, I sure hope so, I'm one of them.

V: Now, would you take time out before the next record to explain to us about how you got into your new show and everything. How did it all begin?

C: Well, it went pretty much like this; I don't know if you fellas know it. Practically all the packaging is done in Los Angeles, except for the short wave, and that comes from Washington, like the President's speech, or different sports events. It started due to the fact that they had received several letters from service men requesting a female voice over the air. They haven't had a girl, from what I understand, since World War II when they had G.I. Jill. They said, 'Okay, we're going to find a girl.' They started doing voice tapes and I had a friend who was at Armed Forces that day and he said, 'Hey, I know a girl who I'm sure would love to come in and do this. Can she come in and make a tape, too? They said, 'Yes.' I went and did a tape, and a few weeks later I got a call saying that I got selected for Armed Forces Radio. I must admit, I was pretty bad in those early shows. I'd never been a disc jockey before, or anything at all like this, but that was my learning period. It's exciting knowing AFRTS operates 300 radio and 43 military TV stations serving US personnel around the world.

V: Well, it's fantastic and I'm sure that throughout the remainder of my tour, and I'm sure the story is the same for the rest of the troops out here, we'll be looking forward to it every night. It comes on at 9:00, and is aired twice daily.

C: Yeah, it sure does. I love this show. It's probably the greatest thing I've done in my whole career.

V: Here's an interesting note you might think about. I had one particular article that I read about you, that you were to combat Hanoi Hannah, which was a comedy show in essence, but the thing is, right now you are blocking out Hanoi Hannah because we're on the same frequency.

C: Well, that's great. I'm all for that!

V: How about some music?

C: Okay, this is one of my favorites. It's the Moody Blues . . . Oh no, you know what it is? It's Johnny Rivers, and *The Poor Side of Town* . . . (song is played). That's a real big one for Johnny.

V: It is. I've heard a great deal about it from the States. I received letters from the States: "Hey, have you heard *The Poor Side of Town?*"No, I haven't heard it yet, and about a month later I'll hear it.

C: Hey, it's really groovy; I like that one.

V: Now that your show is on, I guess we'll be hearing a lot of the latest records.

C: Yeah, but I play a lot of songs besides the top 40. Pretty much the things I'm playing today are what I think are the best of the top 40, and some of the old ones are my favorites. And I hope all of you out there dig them as much as I do.

V: You just might be the first actress ever to go from movies to a star on the radio. You select a lot of your own songs, isn't that right?

C: Pretty much, sometimes when I'm working, shooting during the day, I'm very fortunate in having a great producer who will pull things for me. Sometimes I'll work all day and I'll run in and do five shows at night, and I'm working all day and all night and I just can't find the time to play all the things, but that doesn't happen too often. I do a lot of country songs, the pop country and jazz. Later on we'll play one of Jimmy Smith's tunes. He's jazz, but his jazz is kind of funky. He'll close the show. I play practically everything but classical because I don't like classical.

V: Before we get into our next record, I'd like to say you're listening to the boss sound of the First Horse, First Cavalry Division in Vietnam. This is Armed Forces Radio . . .

C: (Chris plays, *Go Now.*) Oh, that's groovy sound. I really dig that one. That was done in London. In fact, a friend of mine was responsible for this record. His name is Lord Tim Hudson.

V: What are you going to be doing for the next few days? Going to the places throughout Vietnam?

C: Yes, well, tomorrow morning, which is Friday morning, I'm going to Pleiku and going from there to Danang, and then if I get back to Tan Son Nhut Airbase in time, I'll be coming back here again. I don't know exactly the date. I pretty much know, but they're asking me not to say for security reasons.

V: Yes, I guess it pretty much is classified. Well, where have you been the past few weeks?

C: I spent a couple of days in Saigon where I did many TV and radio spots. I was in the Delta, Nha Trang, Long Binh, Bien Hoa, Thuy Hoa, Quang Tri, Hue, Phnom Penh, Phu Loc, Queson, Phu Bai, Dong Ha, Kontum, An Khe, An Hoa, An Loc, Tay Ninh, and Khe Sanh. Just a few *clicks* from the DMZ to as far south as you can go.

V: Well, what impressed you the most about Vietnam?

C: In general, I was really surprised when I was in Saigon. As all you here have probably gathered by now, I wear mini-skirts all the time. When I came over here, or before I came I thought, 'Wow, I can't wear my mini-skirts in Vietnam. That's all I have with me, so what am I gonna do? Besides wearing my fatigues?' I spoke to someone at the Pentagon, 'Look, is it okay if I do this?' And they said, 'Sure!' But I was leery about the reaction from the civilians. And it's funny seeing them, because they look at me, point, smile, and I don't know what they're saying. Kids ran up to me. They were fascinated by my blonde hair. They couldn't believe I had hair on my arms or pink polish on my finger nails. Anytime several people would collect in one spot—especially where I was— the MPs would move them along for fear of a terrorist grenade. They're very nice about it. When I was walking in the streets they were touching my hair, because I have long blonde hair, and they liked my eye-lashes because I wear mascara and they're long. They're great to me. In fact, one Vietnamese woman spoke English and she walked up to me wearing a silk AoDais. She was beautiful, and she said, 'Thank you so much for coming; we really needed you to come and we hope more girls like you come over because we like you.' I thought that was nice.

V: That's very interesting. How about the troops? What have they been doing? Have they turned out in strong numbers everywhere you've been?

C: You bet! They've been marvelous. I go along and I don't know how some of the fellas can drive the jeeps down the road when I look back and they're not looking at the road. I just don't think they expect to see me when they do. The kind of expressions they use, like 'Hey, was that a woman I saw?'

V: Well, driving is very hazardous as it is. I'm sure that you often add to the problem, but that's a pleasure . . .

C: Time's up, fellas. We'll talk to you all soon . . . Here's a kiss from Chris . . . Bye luv!

With her husband CPT *Ty* Herrington at President Nixon's Inauguration. (Photo by Capitol and Glogan)

With second husband, Roger Hanks at Texas wedding.

9
Falling In Love With Chance

By early spring 1968, I was well entrenched in the war, spending most of my time in the field and little time in Saigon.

To me the real heroines were the nurses ankle deep in blood, trying to put together bits and pieces of bodies and seeing if it was at all possible to make some people whole again.

Maggie (Martha Raye) made frequent trips to Vietnam. She was a very special woman. An honorary colonel in the Green Berets, she entertained troops since World War II. *Maggie* is a comedian whose singing has been underestimated. Known for her big mouth and wit, servicemen knew her for her "big" heart. In Danang, we shared a room. That night, she didn't sleep in her bed because of my continuous coughing and hacking—I had a bad sinus infection. At 11 PM, Jim found *Maggie* in a ratty bathrobe eating cold C-Rations, lima beans and ham. Fashion really isn't important in a war zone.

The following year, on getting back to my hotel after many days in the field, I found *Maggie* talking with three

Green Berets— all officers. She quickly introduced them to
me, saying they were leaving for Camp Jack L. Goodman.
Though I was tired, I agreed to join them. Having a few
people to talk to gave me a lift. One captain, however, by
the time we got to Camp Goodman, tried to wear me down
with his unkind remarks: "Did you get your fill of GIs in
the boonies?" I was in no mood— physically or mentally to
fight off his weird and bitter comments. This other officer,
a lieutenant, noticing my distress, broke into the conversation. In a soft tone, he said, "Miss Noel, I'll show you
around the camp." With that, he rescued me from the
tyrant.

Looking back into these scattered memories, I must admit I was impressed by my rescuer, Ty. I still remember
how he wore his green beret. He was so handsome!

We strolled around Camp Goodman, and I found myself
enjoying his company. He took me to his living quarters.
On opening the door to his room, I immediately noticed a
portrait of a beautiful woman in a silver frame. "Oh, she's
really pretty. Is she your wife?"

"No, my mother wishes she was," he answered matter-
of-factly.

I believed him. He was Clyde Berkley Herrington of
Mullins, N.C.— his nickname, Ty. Sensitive and protec-
tive, he was also handsome, and acted like a real southern
gentleman.

He proceeded to show me his weapons, and seemed
especially proud of his pistol. Also proud of the Green
Berets, he moved toward a small poster with the Special
Forces Creed.

"Could I read it to you?" he asked in a soft voice.

"Sure," I answered, somewhat subdued. I stood next to
him, looking at his serious expression:

I am an American Forces Soldier!
A Professional!
I am a volunteer, knowing well the hazards of my profession.
I serve with the memory of those who have gone before me: Roger's
Rangers, Francis Marion Mosby's Rangers, The First Special Service
Forces, and Ranger Battalions of World War II, The Airborne Ranger
Companies of Korea.

I pledge to uphold the honor and integrity of all that I am in all that I do.

I am a professional soldier: I will teach and fight wherever my Nation requires.

I will strive always to excel in every art and artifice of war.

I know that I will be called upon to perform tasks in isolation, far from familiar faces and voices: with the help and guidance of my God I will conquer my fears and succeed.

I will keep my mind and body clean, alert, and strong; for this is my debt to those who depend upon me.

I will not fail those with whom I serve.

I will not bring shame upon myself or the Forces.

I will maintain myself, my arms and my equipment in an immaculate state as befits a Special Forces Soldier.

I will never surrender though I be the last; if I am taken I pray that I have the strength to spit upon my enemy.

My goal is to succeed in any mission— and to live to succeed again.

I am a member of my Nation's chosen soldiery; God grant that I may not be found wanting, that I will not fail this sacred trust.

On finishing the reading, he looked at me. An expression of melancholy covered his face. I said nothing.

Driving around in Ty's jeep, I couldn't forget the words of that nasty captain, "What the f . . . are you doing here? I know what Maggie's doing here. She's been with the Green Berets a long time." He made me wonder again what I was doing there. Most of the enlisted men and officers accepted me and understood my mission— not this bastard. (Later I learned he had been caught stealing from special funds—trading steaks and guns and other things on the black market.)

As the evening went on, I was enjoying Ty. It was really strange for me to be with a Green Beret or any man for that matter. In the few hours we spent together a whole new life was starting. When he dropped me off at my room in Saigon, he asked me to dinner the next night. That was my first date in Vietnam.

We met early, went to a French restaurant, and talked endlessly. He was a special kind of person. He brought me back to my room early and in a very clumsy way, kissed me. As we kissed, I could feel our bodies tremble. Though I asked myself what I was doing there, I couldn't break away.

Over the next few days, I realized I had fallen in love with him. We dated, ate at the best French-Vietnamese restaurants and generally had a great time together. My favorite was a floating restaurant which specialized in garlic crab and corn soup. As terrorists threw hand grenades aboard, we named it the *Claymore Cafe* (after Claymore Mines). I talked about my friends in Hollywood and he told me about the orphans he was helping. Before I left for the States, we had our picture taken together.

As time went by, I noticed that Ty was bothered by my wearing mini-skirts and my friendliness with enlisted men. I then started to wear slacks.

"Love is blind." Well, I fell in love for the first time.

And so began our storybook romance— the dashing young Green Beret officer and blonde Hollywood actress. We had incredible nights together driving through the dark streets of Saigon, in an open jeep, my hair flying, and Ty with a drink in his hand, singing songs.

He introduced me to his friends, and fed me thick steaks. I didn't like steak, but I didn't tell him. We cooked dinners, lit candles and drank wine. It was so romantic. We toured Saigon churches and temples. Throughout, he showed an incredible need for a woman and I an equal need for a man, especially one with whom I could talk. I was ready for romance, and the man-of-my-life had finally appeared.

One day he said, "Come on, I've got a surprise for you. We're going into Cambodia."

"Oh Ty, we're not supposed to do that. We could get shot going there. Oh hell, let's go," I said, answering the challenge.

We went by helicopter, just the two of us and the pilot. While watching the sunset from the air, Ty turned to me and asked, "Will you marry me?" "What did you say?" I yelled above the noise of the chopper. "Will you marry me!" I caught my breath and whispered "Yes."

The next day I left him behind to go to the highlands. "The road to romance is bumpy"; ours was marked with separations.

The Montagnards

I always enjoyed spending time in the fields watching Green Berets train native strike forces and drinking rice wine with Montagnards. These primitive people, who hunted for game with crossbows and played music for me on cymbals of many tones.

With Captain Smith as my escort, I also visited with the Montagnards (Yards, for short), natives who had never seen a wheel much less a white woman. These mountaineer hillbillies, aboriginal Malaysians— not Chinese, Vietnamese or Cambodian, were disliked by the VC and Vietnamese who called them "Mois"—dirty savages or baboons. Those near Kontun had a lot of tuberculosis and a high rate of leprosy.

Of the more than a hundred tribes, the important ones were the Rhade or Bihnar. The men generally wore black vests with bright red and black loin cloths. Some of the women appeared bare-breasted. Their teeth were black from chewing beetle nuts. When they saw me, they stared. The children, on the other hand, were afraid. Some, however, smiled with their black teeth when I gave them chewing gum.

They loved to give me presents of spears, crossbows, brass cymbals and gongs of different sizes.

Carefully walking up a crude ladder, we entered the chief's house. To one side, over a plank that extended to a small child-size structure, was a pile of cut-up meat with blood and insects flying all over it. He was so proud. At his command, the servants brought out their fermented rice wine. We sat in a circle on the floor around a big container. One at a time, we drank from it through a bamboo straw. When the liquid got down to a certain level, more liquid was added to the top again and the next person drank. As I drank, I noticed bugs swimming on the top. Smiling, the chief kept passing it around. His wife smoked a bamboo pipe filled with narcotic tobacco; she stared at me wondering who the hell I was. I never could figure out what she was thinking. Unexpectedly, the chief put a bracelet on my wrist, then gave me a beautiful beaded choker with a silver cross usually worn by virgins. I didn't know what to say!

No doubt about it: one more sip and I'd surely throw up. Just in case, Captain Smith showed me the fence. I didn't want to offend the chief and didn't know how to get out of the situation. So I decided to sing a song. I tried to stand up, but I was too tall. One of the translators produced a little tape recorder. Bent over, in my mini-skirt, I started to sing *Feelin Groovy*, better known as the "59th Street Bridge Song". It sounded just terrible on his recorder.

When I was told they add buffalo blood to the rice wine, I scuttled to the fence.

Press Coverage

My travels throughout Vietnam were usually covered in the press. Here is one of those releases:

"LONG BINH, RVN (199th Inf Bde-IO)— Miss Chris Noel, undoubtedly the best-looking Armed Forces Network disc jockey, recently spent an entire day singing, dancing and joking with more than 1800 GIs of the 199th Light Infantry Brigade.

"Miss Noel, as part of the holiday entertainment visit to Vietnam, performed four shows for men of the 199th— one at the Brigade's main base at Long Binh and one show at each of the 199th's infantry battalion forward fire support-patrol bases. She also visited with soldiers hospitalized at the Brigade dispensary.

"Backed by an Army Special Services band consisting of two electric guitarists and a drummer, Miss Noel invited groups of GIs up on the improvised stages to sing and dance with her. Some of the troop attempts at soloing met with loud hoots and laughter from their buddies and others received genuine applause.

"But it was Miss Noel, wearing the latest stateside mini-skirt, who held the center of attention throughout the day. In addition to the performances, she ate lunch with the troops and autographed countless jungle hats, fatigue caps and pin-up pictures of herself lying on a beach wearing a bikini.

"The green-eyed, blonde entertainer (35-23-35) ignored the heat, blinding sun and dust from resupply helicopters swirling in and out."

I remember Wayne Wolf, a sergeant at Fire Base St. George. He had his buddies grouped together for a picture with me. As he was backing up to get the group into focus, he fell into a 6' hole. Going down, he yelled, "The rest is history."

In 1968, back in the Central Highlands of Vietnam, the 69th Armored 173rd C Company named their M 48 Tank the *Chris Noel*. The first letter of the tank was on the barrel of the gun tube. You see, I was everywhere.

I had lunch only once on the terrace of the Palace Hotel in Saigon. Watching flares and tracers from the rooftops was spellbinding— so unreal! It was like the 4th of July.

On the Mang Yang Pass, bodies of a French Task Force on a suicide mission are buried on the road facing France.

While traveling in the lush countryside, I read this sign: "Imperialistic America, I hate you for the suffering you have caused us. Napalm oozing down the skin, frag wounds from Bouncing Bettys." Other signs, however, did thank the Americans.

On another trip, one of my friends pulled a GI into the helicopter after he had been hit with a Daisy Cutter. His legs had been blown away. Another GI stuck his thumbs into the flesh, trying to stop the flow of blood. Unable to bear the pain, the legless GI gave his last cry: "F . . . breathing." He blew out his air and died.

In the US Army, it is considered disgraceful for soldiers to cry. Yet the ancient Greek heroes of the Trojan wars shed tears without shame or guilt.

At the height of the war, with the anti-war protests and the lack of resolutions at home, the morale of the troops was low. One moment I thought of buying a piece of land in Vietnam to live there after the war; the next moment I'd wonder, "What if the war never ends?"

The Tet Offensive

The 1968 Tet Offensive probably took more American lives than any other battle of the war. For those who participated, it is a time not easily forgotten. I am sure that most of us who were there, directly or indirectly supporting the action, have concluded that though we may have won that battle, the American people at home lost the war for us and for the Vietnamese people. Certainly, America's and South Vietnam's capitulation helped install a government whose tyranny may still be unmatched. Yes, I still live with this thought, especially when I read about the millions of Cambodians and South Vietnamese that were slaughtered.

Because of historical and legendary reasons, the Tet Offensive was a propitious time for the Viet Cong to gather the support of the peasants, women and children. On Radio Hanoi, Hanoi Hannah said, "There will be no survivors".

Village women sent handkerchiefs with the word "peace" embroidered on them to their soldiers unable to return home during Tet.

For me and for the American soldiers it was hard to distinguish between civilians and Viet Cong. I was told to watch the eyes— "The eyes, watch the eyes!" I looked into many eyes, and quickly learned to spot the hatred.

During this time, I began to catch flashes of another side of Ty. A group of guys had just come in from their 100th air mission. Somebody said, "Go out and give them a kiss, Chris", which I did. Furious, Ty stormed out. An hour later, he was all over me with apologies. By now, everyone knew how serious we were. Ty and I were engaged.

One disbeliever was George Skypeck, a patient in the bed next to Ty. They were both wounded during the Tet Offensive. I asked if I could sit on the edge of his bed, which pleased him a great deal. Today, we have become friends. He, of course, is the renowned combat artist and poet. His poem, *Soldier*, is my favorite.

In the immediacy of life and death, our romance had become everybody's romance— Chris Noel and "one of them." With the exception of time spent taping my shows, I was one of the guys. I no longer needed their love and adoration to validate my existence. I saw the faces, felt their fear, and wondered why they were all being condemned for being there, no matter whose fault or why. In some bizarre warp in time, these were the real heroes.

Nashville

Back in the States, between my work preparing shows and other professional commitments, I kept rather busy. Many times, however, I thought of my romance with Ty and how everything went by so fast. It had love, gentleness, serenity, and passion; it also had war, guns, the military, hippies and show business. Yes, it had everything— everything combined. Just as Robert Duvall said in *Apocalypse Now*, "It's exhilarating, it's exciting". Our romance was all that, except for one thing: it went by quickly. Now, in Nashville, while working with Fred Foster, owner of Monument Records, I got the surprise of my life. Not only was Ty married; he also had two little girls. The picture of the woman in the silver frame was his wife after all. Ty had finally admitted the truth to me in a letter.

My next surprise was to answer the doorbell of my house and to find Ty standing on the doorsteps. I tried to close the door on him but failed. He convinced me to let him in because he had a lot of things to tell me. After telling me all about himself and his marriage, he said that he had applied for his divorce and that it was imminent. Feeling reassured, I told him he could stay.

After a few days his leave ended. When he left, I was heartbroken. Once again, we continued with our exceptional romance.

"Hi darling," I said to him in a 1968 tape, "I hope this taping is alright. I love you very much and that's something I know that you know. How's General Davis? It's amazing that you are serving under him. To think that you were with his son Steven when he was killed. I am glad to learn that the General has taken you under his wing as another son."

"Anyway, now to get back to how things have been happening. I got a call from Fred. I went to Nashville to overdub my singing. In fact, I re-did all my songs except for three . . . He said my voice was much better and is setting up rehearsals with Joe Taylor. We will be recording at The Barn. I went to Felice and Boudleaux Bryant's house and picked up some barbecue . . . I met Fred again for ten minutes and he played your recording. I must tell you Ty, I flipped out of my head. It is so good. The things he's done to it; you're going to love it. Ty, you're going to be so happy. I tell you, he's making you sound like Andy Williams; and me, I sound like Barbara Streisand—ha, ha! The next day, Fred came over and picked Boudleaux and myself up and we went to the studio and saw Charlie. Remember Charlie McCoy? he said to say hello to you. It's getting cold in Nashville. He says he keeps his houseboat out on Hickory Lake. Just like Mickey Newberry . . . Anyway, we started recording all my songs over again. The best one is *Doll House* backed by Mr. and Mrs. Smith. That's going to be my first single. Now as much as I love *I've Got To Have You* by Kris Kristofferson (one of his first songs) that's probably my third favorite now, because it's just too fast. Boudleaux, Felice and I had dinner. It was really good. We watched *Cat Ballou* on TV and went to sleep.

"The first two nights I couldn't sleep. I was such a wreck going in to record. You can imagine how it was. I let you down because I didn't write you those days, but I knew you would understand, knowing how I get when it comes to my recording. I really can't think about much of anything. Fred said, 'It'll get easier and easier and easier each time.' You know, but I'll tell you he's got a lot of plans for you and me. I know that much. He said that if we wanted to come and live in Nashville, he'd see about getting me a job. He said, 'You'd make a great promotion man if you wanted to do something like that.' This morning I got up and listened to your tape that had come in the mail. Fred is such a gentleman. He has never gotten out of line with me at all. You know, I wear your bracelet with C.B. Herrington on it. He'd look at Boudleaux and say, 'You wouldn't think she was crazy about Ty Herrington would you?' We're very lucky to be as close to him as we are. I love you and I'll send you another tape tomorrow."

On another tape, I told him what I thought of being in love with a married man:

"It's depressing knowing you're still married, especially when people ask when we're getting married and I have to say I don't know . . . I would rather people just didn't know. Now, about Tiger, my little kitten. Tiger was killed by a car . . . When I picked her up, she had only a couple of breaths—breathed just a little bit and then died . . . You say that in a 60 hour period you only had four hours of sleep but that when you're in the field you get plenty of sleep because you go to bed early. It doesn't sound to me like you're getting much sleep and you had better take care of yourself . . . I still haven't found out when I'm leaving for the Pacific . . .

"If I remember correctly, it is pretty swampy where you are. I just don't want you to catch pneumonia and get real sick. I don't know if the silicone spray I sent for your boots will help at all to keep the water out or if the powder helps the feet from getting infected. If you need anything, if you have any problems like sores on your arms or anything like that, tell me and I'll get the right kind of medicine for you, OK? I told you about my Winston commercial running, didn't I? And it's running quite a bit, because I hardly ever watch TV and I know I've seen it three times, which means I'll be getting residual money from it. I just got another $400 in from the motion picture, but I don't know why I can't get enough money saved. I certainly better do something about it. And I'm not spending money either. I'm really not. I told you about the letter I received from General Davis . . . It would be groovy if he came to our wedding . . . "

My Wedding

The romance that started on the battlefield of Vietnam turned into a marriage in Florida.

My girlfriend Patty Olsen Rautbord gave us the wedding at her Miami home. BG General Franklin Davis was best man, and fellow Green Berets, SGT Billy Kessinger and LT Richard English were also present along with Boudleaux Bryant, and Ty's brother, Bill. Patty was my matron of honor; my sister Trudie, and my girlfriends Mary Taylor, Eileen, Felice, Lynne Baldwin and Christina Campanelli were bridesmaids.

The press covered my beautiful wedding to a paratrooper who was wounded three times while serving 18 months in Vietnam.

On our honeymoon, we went to Washington, D.C. for the inauguration of President Nixon. God, Ty was so handsome in his dress blues! I did not tell anyone, however, that Ty had become unnerved since being back in the States. I knew that women had to put up with all kinds of things. Since I wanted my marriage to work, I sought ways to help him. Ty was leaving the service.

One of his problems was that he couldn't get a job anywhere. He had a college background and had done various things before going into the Service. However, most servicemen returning in the late 60's weren't considered heroes. Employment was scarce for veterans.

"You were in Vietnam? Well, we don't have a job for you."

"Hell no, I won't give you a job, sucker."

I saw it happen many times to so many veterans. It really burned me up, and I must admit it hurt me deeply.

I continued to do my radio show, still in love with that man who'd been in Vietnam and couldn't get a job, though he was very intelligent and bright. He did a couple of recordings, *A Gun Don't Make A Man*, and *When The Green Berets Come Home*, but neither was successful, even though I played his songs on my show. Things were not going well, and this awareness preyed on our minds. I began to worry.

Ty's Behavior

As time passed, I found Ty having more and more difficulty dealing with my career. He hated my being in front of the public and didn't like my being the center of attention. Yet, basically, that's what attracted him to me.

He had no job and resented being looked down upon, not being a hero— a shattering blow to a lot of veterans. Soon, we began to have big problems. I wasn't working as much, and during our vacation in Hawaii, I had a miscarriage. I remember: blood everywhere. I washed the sheets and hung them out on the balcony to dry because I was so embarrassed. When I went to bring them inside, I found the wind had blown them away. I felt incredibly sad because I really wanted Ty's child. Ty was very concerned and sweet to me during this crisis.

Fred, Felice, and Boudleaux encouraged us to move to Hendersonville, Tennessee, where all the country music celebrities lived, with the hope of working in Nashville. Ty wanted to be a teacher more than anything, and needed a job—any job, and our friends offered to help— all to no avail.

In Tennessee I couldn't find work in movies; in Hollywood, Ty couldn't find work, period!

Suddenly, he started pulling his gun on me. Whenever anything didn't go right, he'd freak out at the drop of a hat. That's when I first became afraid of him.

I was deeply depressed and finally went to a psychiatrist and requested he put me in a hospital.

I was talking to the doctor when Ty rushed in. Ten minutes later, the doctor left and came back with the release papers.

"I don't want to leave," I complained.

"You have to leave," the doctor said. "Your husband is disturbing the hospital."

On the way home, I asked Ty to go see the doctor on his own, which he did. After a couple of visits, his doctor took me aside. "Ty is a manic-depressive paranoid schizophrenic and he needs to be committed."

I couldn't believe it. I knew Ty had mental problems. "Everyone thought Ty was just fine; now you're telling me I have to commit him."

How was I going to do this? I was tired, stressed and sick myself.

Ty's First Suicide Attempt?

Several of my friends, on hearing I was marrying a Green Beret I had just met in Vietnam, tried to dissuade me from going through with the marriage. One of these was Christina, who did not hide her shock. Even after seeing how much Ty and I were in love— we had spent a lot of time in her company and she had seen the great affection between us. She, of course, saw Ty differently than I did. When she told me she saw him as a little boy in a man's body, I did not agree with her simply because I did not want to believe it. After all, mine was not a fantasy. Now that all these things were happening, I can see how right Christina was and how wrong— no, downright stupid— I was! However, as they say, "Love is blind."

At one of our parties, Ty said some very cruel things to me. As usual, I would respond by putting on a happy face. Christina neither liked the way he talked to me nor his pouting. Noticing his behavior, she took me aside, but to no avail.

At another party Ty became abusive in front of our friends. Embarrassed, I took off without saying anything to him. Christina called Ty to tell him I was okay. He ordered her to tell him where I was or he would kill himself. She then heard a gunshot and the phone drop. I called the police, and we went to my house. Ty was not there, but we saw the bullet hole. All of my mini-skirts were cut in half. The photographs of me were slashed. There was no doubt he had done this. But, where was he?

Christina was sure Ty was sick. She also knew that there was no way that the two of us could have a normal relationship. When I told her I was going back to him, she suggested that I stay away. "You need to be with a healthy mind, Chris," she said. On hearing those words, I stopped to ponder. After several hours, I finally decided she was right, that I should stay away for an indefinite period of time. Christina, of course, suggested that I stay at her apartment.

Needing to get some of my clothes, I decided not to take the chance of going to my house and finding Ty there. I called his commanding officer at Fort McArthur. On being assured he was at his job, I rushed to the house. To my disappointment and dismay, there was Ty, in full uniform. On seeing me, he was as nice as pie— oh, I can't tell you! He told me how much he loved me, that he would never act as crazy as in the past, etc. Well, I found myself melting like butter. Before I knew it, I had said I would stay and remain with him. That afternoon, we had the most passionate love of our lives. While we were enjoying that love, I felt an inner anxiety. I didn't want it to end, though I knew it would, and it did.

Months later, in fear of my life, I left Ty for the second and last time.

Suicide

I arranged for Ty to go to my attorney's office where I called to speak with him. I was afraid to be in his presence.

"I'm sorry. It'll never happen again," he said. "I really understand. I don't blame you after the way I've been. Don't you love me anymore? I've changed. Please stay. We can make it work. Please don't leave me," he continued, his voice softening. When I did not answer, he became furious. "You f . . . whore, I'll get you. You won't come back? I'll find you. One of these days you'll be on a stage somewhere, and you know I always have a gun with me— and you know I'll find you and you know what I'll do. I'll kill you! You're the only person who really knows me and what I'm capable of doing."

"Ty, you'll never frighten me again," I said resolutely.

Next morning, Boudleaux called and told me that Ty had shot himself in the head. When he couldn't tell me more, I called Mark Clark Bates and Tex Ritter, who were Ty's employers.

"Chris, I don't think you understand," Mark said in a comforting tone, "his brains are shot out. Even if he lives, he'll be a total basket case. He won't be able to see, talk, do anything. His brains are gone."

"Is he still alive! Is he still alive?"

"He's breathing."

Not wanting me to go alone, Eileen quickly called the airport and made reservations to fly to Nashville.

At the hospital, my attorney came over to tell me that Dixie, Ty's friend, wanted to see me.

I asked the sobbing woman to walk to the chapel with me. She told me that Ty had shot himself in her bathroom, and that she and Ty had been lovers. She looked at me with tears in her eyes. I put my arms around her and cried. After a few moments, she told me that the night before Ty had taken a whole bottle of tranquilizers. (She has supposedly later denied this.)

When I was finally allowed by his bedside, I talked to him, telling him that in spite of everything I still loved him. Though he could not talk, I noticed he was hearing me because he signaled me with his hand. "Yes," I repeated, "I still love you very much, and I know that deep down, you love me just as much. I will always love you."

How strange? Even though I was saying those things, I assumed that God would do the right thing, because never once did I say I hoped he would live in that condition.

A couple of hours later, while in the corridor, I saw a machine brought into Ty's room. I knew he had died.

I went back to see him— this time with Boudleaux. I could feel Ty's spirit lingering around his body, and after a few seconds, going away. (I know, it's strange; but I felt his spirit separating and depart. I just felt numb).

At the home of Boudleaux and Felice, with Dixie upstairs, I was downstairs crying and yelling that Dixie should not be present at the funeral. Instead, it was me who was not allowed to be present. Ty's parents had made it clear that I was the Hollywood harlot who had lured their son into show business and was responsible for his death.

In any event, I quickly contacted Martha Raye and others, and was able to arrange with the general of Fort Bragg for a military funeral. Ty was to be in dress blues with his green beret and his body to be transported to his parents' home for burial.

With sleeping pills, I was able to barely survive. Since I wasn't allowed at the funeral, I was able (with the help of Fred, Boudleaux, Felice, Dane and several Nashville

friends) to have a memorial service of my own. It was
Christmas and I was alone again. My fairytale romance
tragically ended, together with my dreams of a family of
my own. The only thing I had was a St. Christopher neck-
lace inscribed, "My love for life, Ty." It matched the one he
still wore around his neck. I also found in his wallet this
prayer:
   "God, grant me the serenity to accept the things I cannot
change, the courage to change the things I can, and the
wisdom to know the difference." Lost people do live lost
lives.

   Richard Patrick of Royal Oak, Michigan, served under
Ty in the 199th Light Infantry Division in Bien Chon, Chair
Hiep and Nah Ba: "Ty was one of the most impressive
people I ever met. I really felt confident around him. You
knew he wouldn't tell you to do anything to get your head
chopped off. He was a charger . . . "
   Joe Cozzo, a police officer in Cambridge, Massachusetts,
flew a (Loch) gunship from Phu Bai to Camp Eagle and
Camp Davis: "No one else knew you but everyone was so
happy you and Ty were getting married. We didn't realize
he was so well-known. I read how he died and that he was
a folk singer and an entertainer. He was a good leader—
not the kind that lead by beating people up. He was
whatever makes a good leader."
   Bob Jacobson, a staff officer, told me that Ty was "very
popular, charismatic, daring and competent in Vietnam.
He was a damned good company commander."
   And BG Franklin Davis wrote: "I guess none of us ever
gets to know a friend well, and certainly all I saw of Ty was
the one dimension he chose to disclose and that is how I
will remember him. But I know for a fact from what I have
seen of men in general during my long time in this business and also from what I have seen of the mental cases we
do deal with, that there was probably nothing any of us
could have done to prevent Ty taking this course once he
embarked on his particular line of gloom and despair. Help
in these instances has to come from professionals, the ultimate act of destruction can be triggered by virtually any

crisis the individual feels he cannot handle, and the friends and loved ones involved can no more alter this course than we can alter the course of the sun.

"Again, our hearts go out to you, and of course to Ty's family and your own too, and to your many other friends. We will always remember Ty at his best—he made this a better place."

Several weeks later, I contacted General Davis, who was now stationed at the Pentagon, wanting to find out what was being done to help the returning veterans. I told him that we gave them combat training prior to going into action, but that it appeared to me that little was being done to prepare them for their return. Candidly remorseful, he answered that there weren't any real big plans for the repatriation.

In looking around, I was told that unlike the veterans of other wars, many Vietnam veterans were in jails, had committed suicide, or died from drug and alcohol related problems. Furthermore there are an untold number of walking wounded; their deaths are reported from mysterious ways— sleeping deaths with booze and pills at the side of their beds. There is a cancer which killed, among others, General Davis, who died of a tumor in the brain, as Mrs. Davis herself believes. Yes, Agent Orange!

America's Creed

"I believe in the United States of America as a government of the people, by the people, for the people; whose just powers are derived from the consent of the governed; a democracy in a Republic; a sovereign Nation of many sovereign States; a perfect Union, one and inseparable; established upon those principles of freedom, equality, justice and humanity for which American patriots sacrificed their lives and fortunes. I, therefore, believe it is my duty to my country to love it; to support its constitution; to obey its laws; to respect its flag; and to defend it against all enemies."

A scroll, with these words inscribed, was given to me upon graduating from Palm Beach High School. It has meant so much to me over the years.

Words— Without Meaning, Without End
Vietnam . . . Back and forth: war, blood, raw emotions, wrapped bodies, pain on men's faces: pain, pain, pain; scared, sniper fire, helicopter crash, mortars crashing around me, sleeping alone in a big trailer, mortar shaking me out of bed, scared, fright, children maimed, napalm, men's faces blown off, double-triple amputees.

Blood, blood, blood!

Tired, drained, sick, throw up, keep moving, don't think, give, smile, be pretty, never cry, smile, pain, too much, can't go on, I have to, they need me, smile.

In a few more weeks, you'll be stateside, smile, pain, scared, cries in the night, nightmares, shadows, rats, mosquitos, planes, noises, Howitzers, guns, noise, noise, tired, sick, keep going, you can do it, fix your make-up, sing, pretty, the boys just want someone to care.

A quiet sensitive man who's married and never tells me for months, asks me to marry him, yes, yes, how romantic, war and love, proposal in a helicopter over Cambodia, off-limits, high, driving about after curfew in the middle of the night, have to be up by 6 AM to go out into the field.

Back and forth to the States, I can rest, it'll be alright, I'll be home, why do people act like they hate me? Are they right? Am I wrong? Am I just a toy being used by my country? They don't understand our men are hurting, they need help. Firebases, aircraft carriers, graves registration where all the dead boys are, hospitals, landing zones, tired, smile, smile.

Love, a man, his arms around me. I need it so much—happy, fairytale romance, love to erase the horrors, he understands, don't have to talk about it, jealous? No, it'll be alright, crazy? All men in war are crazy, so am I to be here.

Married, why does he talk about death so much? Smoking grass, never crying, he's getting crazier, I'm now fighting back, pulling me across the room by my hair, too often a gun to my head, I file for divorce, he kills himself, my shock, he really killed himself, don't feel guilty, people say, one after another, don't feel guilty, good thing you weren't there, he would have killed you.

So tired!

Happiness!

Happiness?

10
Childhood Memories

I lived a lifetime during the Sixties. In my late twenties, I had already been a successful beauty contestant, a co-star in popular movies, a highly paid New York model and had a few romances with Hollywood leading men. I even fell in love and got married.

During my years in and out of Vietnam, I began to feel the effects of the war— physically, emotionally and mentally. On a couple of occasions, I had to hold on to a light post on a New York street corner until my head stopped spinning. I began having headaches and heart palpitations, even my vision became impaired. From physical symptoms like warm and moist skin, increased fatigue, muscular weakness and rapid beating of the heart, to the psychological-like restlessness, emotional instability, depressions, sleeplessness and a lot of irritability, I began doubting my being able to make it. My doctors prescribed sedatives, told me to rest, to relax, that nothing was wrong with me. I begged for referrals to psychologists and other specialists, but to no avail. Aside from seeking proper therapy, I began to delve into my past to gain some answers and explanations.

When I was four years old, my real father came into the bathroom to relieve himself while I was soaking in the tub. I was amazed. Shocked, my mother spoke loudly to my father about this action. My mother never appeared nude or even bare-breasted in front of me. My stepfather too was always dressed when I saw him in the mornings before leaving for school. At a local movie theater with my cousin Sonny, an old man came in and sat down next to me. Before I knew it, he was trying to seduce me; but I knew that was wrong. In my teens, I was babysitting for an infant boy. On feeling the wetness, I decided to change him. As I took off the wet diaper, wow, right in the face. That's when I began to really know the difference between men and women.

Life was different then. I always tried so hard to please my mother because I wanted her to be proud of me. I remember walking on Clematis Street, my sister on my mother's right and I on her left. I did something I wasn't supposed to do and started crying. My mom said, "Don't you cry, what will people think?" As she was holding my hand, she dug her long fingernails into my palms— an early lesson in not showing my real feelings in public. As a result, I worked very hard to stay the good, sweet little girl. I always felt very close to my mom, maybe because I was born on her birthday, because she's her special self.

Though many episodes created stress, Ty's suicide was the most difficult. Dr. Albert Cain, a University of Michigan professor of psychology, said that the stress from suicide can produce physical exhaustion, migraines, hypertension, ulcers, colitis and even lead to death.

Four years old.

With mother, Louise Botz.

Press photo. (MGM)

With the Duke and Duchess of Windsor.

11
My Texan

I always loved the holidays, so I could go to Florida and lie in the sun at the beach. I craved it and thought about it so often when exhausted, tired, confused and in need of rest. Show business has so many ups and downs.

While recuperating at home in West Palm Beach, Patty and Bobby Rautbord invited me to a New Year's party given by Marge and Irv Cowan, the owners of the Diplomat Hotel in Hollywood, Florida, at their lavish home.

At the dinner table, I sat between Jacqueline Susann and Steve Alaimo. I was having a great conversation with Steve—a neat guy; but Jacqueline, on the other hand, kept putting her hand on my knee and thigh. To get away, I asked Steve to dance— which was the start of a very sweet and healthy new romance, one I really needed. Because he was booked at the Caribe Hilton in Puerto Rico, I went with him to rest in the sun and watch him perform at night. I needed support and Steve gave it to me. He was a singer and a record producer who was very much involved in his music career. I began to make plans to return to New York and restart my career in modeling and commercials. To this day, I think that he started me back on the survival route with his kindness and thoughtfulness.

Life in New York was torturous. Because of the Valium I was taking, I could not even finish my nightly prayers. In the morning, I'd be angry because I couldn't finish the prayers. It was as though something, some energy force, came in between. I remember, even in Vietnam, toward the end, of my tours, I would hear Martha Raye walk by and say, "God bless you" to the guys, and I couldn't say it. I would look at her and marvel at the fact that she could do that. "What's wrong with me? I can't say 'God bless you.' And I'd just sit there and dig my fingernails into my hands because I couldn't do it. It's as though something comes in and messes up the psyche. It's not just with me; it's with a lot of veterans as well. It could be a problem of the subconscious. "If there is a God, then how can He let this happen?" And yet, deep in my heart, I believed there is a God. But, why is this happening, if you're supposed to be a loving God? Everything I learned as a child, I was now beginning to question and to doubt. At night, distorted and dead bodies kept flashing in my head. We all have pictures in our minds of dying peaceably with our hands down at our sides, just the perfect specimen of the dead body. These bodies were all distorted; they were hard to pick up— an arm sticking out one way, a leg another, and a head another. I kept saying, "Come on, you have to go to sleep; you have to get these things out of your head." Instead of thinking peaceful thoughts, the mind recreates our hell.

I tried everything to get rid of those distortions, including praying and chanting so I could sleep. I would take L-Tryptophan, an amino acid for people who need to relax and sleep; I also took salts, a homopathic remedy, good for anxiety and depression, because I don't remember ever having those kinds of thoughts before I went to Vietnam. I never did. Before Vietnam, I was happy; I had everything. My head was clear. I never worried about meditating nor about praying. I had a fabulous life, fabulous boyfriends, fabulous parties, and ate at the best of restaurants. I was very, very happy.

Skip Ward, who had introduced me to Jack Jones and was one of Hollywood's golden boys, once commented, "Hey, how come you always smile?" Because I was happy, feeling good, and it's amazing how all of a sudden all of that can be gone— robbed?

I always hoped and prayed that tomorrow would bring me a new and meaningful life. My matchmaker friends, Patty and Bobby took me to a party given by Don and Shirley Aronow, owners of famous racing boats, at their beautiful home in Coral Gables.

Don Aronow designed the "Cigarette" for the man who wants the Ferrari sports car image— "Hot, fast, lean, sleek, sexy, always ready— the ideal mistress for any man." Don in turn introduced me to Roger Hanks, who had forgotten we had met two years earlier when Roger won the Key West Off Shore Powerboat Race. When our eyes met, I knew a new life was in store for me. Roger was very attentive. Before the evening was over, I knew we would eventually marry.

Though about eleven years my senior, Roger was ruggedly handsome, lots of curly brown hair— a Wichita Falls Texan. We spent some time together and we drove back to West Palm Beach to meet my parents. Ironically, we were booked on the same flight to Dallas where I was moving to start my singing career in the new progressive country music scene taking place in Austin and Dallas. Within a few weeks, we were engaged.

In Dallas, life was lonely. I made the rounds of publishers and agents, but my heart was in Midland with the man I loved. I quit my singing career and went to join Roger, and we simply got married. Everything was great at long last!

Soon, however, I learned that Roger was accident-prone and that he had a teenage son who hated me from the very first time we met.

My new husband had an innate desire for speed— all kinds; he also had alcohol problems. He was in several racing boat accidents across the country; he even piled up his Maserati and his Ferrari burned in his garage. He came close to death so many times that I had to believe someone was watching over him.

My new life was spent making the rounds of hospitals, alcohol centers, and trying to be a housewife. To add to the problems, his son broke his neck diving into the shallow end of the pool when he was stoned. What had I gotten myself into? As if I didn't have enough problems of my own. I started spending money.

On the day I put Roger on a plane for the Hazelton Treatment Center in Minnesota, I had to drive his younger son Preston to the hospital to have his stomach pumped.

I should have had a clue to my future. A few weeks before we got married, Roger was testing his famous Texas Orange racing boat which blew up in front of my eyes, shooting him high into the air. With pieces of the boat flying all around, he fell back into the water. I thought he was dead. His mechanic, who was in a second boat, screamed at me to get in, and we raced to Roger's rescue. As we pulled him into the boat, I smelled alcohol on his breath. Shaken, I took one valium. On our way to the hospital, I had a premonition not to go into this marriage— the same kind of feeling I got before marrying Ty. However, I didn't heed that clear admonition.

Earlier, he had shown me a clipping from the *New York Post*, of a photo of his "Cigarette" Racing Boat in a crash, it's nose sticking out of the other side of the hull of a Hatteras Check Point Boat, the word "Blonde" clearly written across the side, and the caption: "Two ships that didn't pass in the night"— another clue I conveniently overlooked. I was in love! Can you imagine, at my age? Not that falling in love is unusual at any age. I wanted the stability. I wanted this marriage to work.

In Midland, we had friends— Monette and Willy B. Wilson, Jeanette and Bill Probandt. To stay busy and feel useful, I joined the Symphony Guild, the Ballet Guild, Republican Women, Salvation Army Board, and the Petroleum Woman's Club. I even took classes at Midland College. With all these activities, I found time to start a modeling school and the Noel Cosmetic Company— both rather successful ventures. I wanted to stay busy.

There were other things I enjoyed during my marriage to Roger, who had many interesting friends. One of my favorites was Jim Hall, who, together with a group of Texas investors, put together his new *Chapparal* car driven to victory by Al Unser. That car was the only winner of the triple crown: Riverside, California 500, the Poconos 500, and the biggest of them all, the Indianapolis 500. I will never forget the thrill in running down to the winner's circle and standing there with Roger and Al in front of thousands of Indy fans.

During those six years of marriage, we lived in four homes. We moved from a beautiful house in Racquet Club to a town house and then to another superb dwelling on Saddle Club Drive. I did all the decorating to make a showplace for Roger and me. My stepson Preston lived with us. Never having had a brother or a son of my own, I tried my best to help him and to get him to love me; but, he was just impossible.

Unexpectedly, I began having female problems, resulting in a hysterectomy. It left a scar in my soul because I knew I could never have a child of my own.

Roger's oil business brought us to Santa Fe— a beautiful and charming city, clean and exciting, with very creative, artistic, interesting and well-read people. We decided to buy a second house on Tano Road which was on the top of a mountain. I felt like I was in heaven for the first time. I had everything! (I remember thinking those same words when I was with Ty— oh how the past continues its haunting!)

There was a tremendous view of the Sangre de Cristo Mountains, a master bedroom separated from the other bedrooms by a huge open area containing a swimming pool, large dining room, Mexican Talavera tiles, Mexican light fixtures, and yes, tin work for the valances and switchplates by Emilio and Senaida Romero. Best of all, at night I could see our large American flag. With the flood lights, it looked even more beautiful as it unfurled in the mountain breeze.

No matter where we looked, we had spectacular views of the lights of Los Alamos and Santa Fe, mesas and mountains, to the hulking outline of Sandia Peak. Living on this mountaintop should have brought me happiness. It didn't.

My headaches and breathing problems continued to torment me. Roger kept on yelling at me, probably because his many accidents were catching up to him and he was taking it out on me.

One night, I received a call from his oldest son, Roger Jr., who told me to meet his dad at the hospital. In showing his son how to pick up a rattler, it turned and bit him. How Roger flew his own plane back to Santa Fe, I'll never know.

With antidote dripping into his system, Roger looked at me with guilt. He fought the doctors because he wanted to leave. The doctors insisted he stay. Since this was a matter of life or death, I refused to sign the release, which made him violently mad. To appease his father, Roger Jr. signed the papers. We went home where I stayed up all night watching him toss and turn and sweat, wondering if he would make it.

The next day, I read in the local paper that Alicia Albelson had advertised a metaphysical class on "Polarity and Color Healing." I had hoped it would free me from my dilemma. I did not have emotional security.

Realizing that Roger's life was no longer my responsibility, I started working on understanding my own life, and became ambivalent about my marriage, in spite of the fact that I loved him. He reminded me of a big, lovable teddy bear. Yet, I began to give serious thought to a divorce.

I arranged for the two of us to visit with Alicia, but he refused. On telling him I had been to a divorce attorney, he agreed to go— one time only. With Alicia, he talked about the business man who kicks his dog. "That's what I do to Chris," he said.

"Roger," I interrupted, "why don't you learn other ways of expressing your anger than taking it out on me? When you're drunk, you're so mean to me!"

On learning that a TV movie was being shot in Santa Fe, I contacted the producer Les Sheldon. Remembering me from Hollywood, he had writers put in a small part for me. Later I found out that years earlier when he was out with Steve McQueen, Les had told Steve he would like to have a date with me. In the movie, I had a scene with Ben Johnson. What a great feeling! I was now back in the motion picture business.

Shortly after my work in the *Wild Ones*, Michael O'Herilly cast me in the O.J. Simpson film, *Detour To Terror*, filmed in Albuquerque. From there, I would fly to Los Angeles staying there Monday to Friday, but was home on Fridays with dinner on the table for Roger, who was piloting his own plane from Santa Fe to Midland and back. While in California, I would stay with Kathy Kersh, who had won the Rheingold contest a year before I was in it.

One night, Roger called to tell me he wouldn't finance my trips to the coast anymore— especially if I was seeking film work. Vehemently, he shouted, "Chris, I know you want a divorce and you've got it." I called my attorney the following morning and quickly filed the papers. Roger and I both cried.

12
From Start To Finish

I've been sensitive and vulnerable all my life. As a result, I have suffered a lot. But I'm dealing with it now, I think. More importantly, I'm talking about it.

I want to be an instrument of God. One of my friends came up and said, "When you smile at people, you heal them. When you smile at people and they're depressed and you say something kind to them you give them a ray of light; you're healing." And that's what I try to do in my own way.

Realizing I needed proper therapy, I looked for and found four therapists who helped me greatly: Shad Meshad, Marcia Weiss, Rod Burk and Don Bush.

Within one year, I went from hardness in my face to a softness. At 40, in fact, I looked younger than I did at 30 when I was carrying all the tightness and tension inside me.

Eric Morris, author of *No Acting Please*, helped me as much as any therapist in Los Angeles.

I had always hated acting classes, but Eric's were very inventive and interesting. The following transcripts are from two group sessions. In each, Eric led us through a process of self-discovery.

"Take One"

E: You look really nice tonight. I would like to ask for some scary feedback. Ask people how they perceive you, especially when you would normally be reluctant or agitated. Ask people's response to you . . . You don't have to go to each person. Ask the people whose feedback is important for you to hear.

C: Do you believe that I'm real most of the time? (I asked this man, who remained silent).

E: Why are you having trouble asking that person?

C: I don't know (I started to cry). Do you think I'm strange because I cry all the time?

M: No.

C: Do you think I'm too pretentious? Do you think I try too hard to look good? (I asked this woman.)

W: No.

E: Ask me that (Eric said sarcastically). I think the way you look is of uppermost importance in your life. I think it takes the place of other considerations and concerns. I think it's misguided. I think on a deeper level, though, you think that it's not the only thing about you that's worthwhile.

C: I think you're right . . . But how is it misguided?

E: I think that you are a very beautiful woman, but I think you're more than that. If you are just beautiful, that would be dull. What else are you? What other interests do you have? What else could you spend your time with, get into, and work on? I think that you don't think you're much else.

C: I'm getting there though.

E: That's why I wanted you to ask me the question. I do think you're too preoccupied in that area . . . So, go on.

C: Do you think I'm too insecure?

W: I think you have a low opinion of yourself. I don't know what *too* insecure means. I do think you're very insecure.

C: (Laughing) Do you think I'm getting there though? Do you think I'm working slowly, or do you think I'm getting there fast?

E: I think you've got the approval you need for yourself; we feel it and I feel good that you're feeling better about yourself every day. I think whatever you're doing is good for you.

C: Do you have any ideas about how I might work toward it?

B: (Billy Hayes from the movie, *Midnight Express*) Yes, try seeing yourself as we see you.

E: Learning something from this, Chris?

C: Do you have any suggestions on how I might feel more secure?

M: Maybe by throwing away your self-image. By throwing away the importance of being free. Just realize that within you there's a great deal of strength regardless of whether your confidence crumbles or not.

E: Ask me that.

B: Don't ask him.

E: Accomplish more. Start out to do things and say, "Hey, look what I've done." Break your own record. Go after some accomplishment, build a track record.

C: I want to ask those of you who have seen me the most: Do you think that when I come in sometimes, I have a hard look on my face? Maybe sometimes the way I wear my hair or my make-up makes me look hard?

E: It's not hard, but it's protectiveness. When you smile you're more open. The protectiveness is insecurity.

C: I used to smile all the time. I just got it the other day about being, "Nancy Nice."

E: It's not the same thing. What we're talking about is protectiveness. It's going away. I think you should feel really good about yourself.

C: I just lost a part the other day because the casting director said I looked hard.

E: Maybe you did.

C: It really brought me down.

T: (Thomas Girvin) If you can decide who you will choose as your friends, choose people who have your best interests in mind, and just trust them. I think you've grown wary from past experiences from people who have given you a lot of shit that you didn't deserve.

E: How do you feel now?

C: Well, I'm just glad I asked that one question. I really needed to know where the hardness comes from. I think I heard some things I really needed to hear.

E: Good. We'll work on it; I think we already have. It's defensiveness and protection— the fear of being hurt. You brace yourself for it.

"Take Two"

E: I'm more involved in an area with you than a specific exercise. What I get from you is a feeling that you feel misunderstood, and that if people knew all the things that have happened to you and what goes on inside, you wouldn't be treated the way you are. That's the general basis. So, what I'd like for you to do is share with us— we'll call it the "History of My Life and the Way I Feel About It." Stand where they can see you . . . over there. Start anywhere. The history of your life doesn't have to have any chronological order.

C: I'll start where I am right now. I am in the process of a divorce, and trying to sort some things out about Vietnam.

E: I want everything to come out. Everything! All of your feelings about these things. I want you to be honest about them and level with us. Okay?

C: When I first went to Vietnam, I didn't know if I was a hawk or a dove or whatever, but when I came back the first time and saw the reaction to me it was . . .

E: What was the reaction?

C: Very hostile.

E: People here?

C: Yes. They were hostile toward me because they thought I was for war, and that's not where my head was. Nobody gives a damn about it and I'm very angry about it.

E: Nobody gives a damn about what?

C: Nobody gives a damn about their feelings. About what everybody went through in Vietnam. There were guys coming back home minus their legs and arms and people would be yelling at them, "Baby Killers!" These were people who had lost half of their bodies. They are still suffering from it and can't talk to anybody about it. I met an

Indian and I said, "Where were you in Vietnam?" And he said "I was in Hue." "You were in a really heavy place." "Yeah, all our guys that came back had to be deprogrammed." "Deprogrammed? How did you get deprogrammed? Who deprogrammed you?" "The Elders did." "You're an Indian, aren't you?" "Yes, I'm a purebred Indian." "Do you know how fortunate you are to be an Indian? Your people take care of their people. We don't take care of our people. We don't take care of each other."

E: Talk about your feelings in that area. You resent it, don't you? You have a lot of anger. Because you feel . . .

C: I feel like I'm getting back into society again and I feel it's very difficult for me. I'm a mature woman and I should be moving on in my life and not be reflecting back. But I know what I've got to do.

E: Do what?

C: I've got to reflect back. I feel that now I have another cause. A cause for me.

E: What's that cause?

C: My cause is to face it and look at the different ways people can be deprogrammed when they have tragedies in their lives. And that's why I'm writing this book. I'm writing this book about my husband's suicide. I'm writing it about my divorce from an alcoholic. I'm writing it about what it's like to be married to a paranoid schizophrenic who put a gun to my head many times. I'm writing about what it was like to be in Vietnam and the feelings from a woman's point of view. What it is like to be in a violent war. I'm writing about all of that, and I am doing it for me. Also I think it will help other people who are trying to deprogram in a lot of different ways. Your class is a deprogramming effort for me.

E: You have a lot of resentment.

C: I have a lot of resentment. I know. I just found out about my anger and my resentment about two weeks ago.

E: Well, I found out about it long before that. I think it's at the root core, the root source of a lot of your difficulties. What I mean and why I've asked you to do this—the "History of My Life" is because I think I know how you feel, and I'm not sure all of it is justified. I think some of it is irrational. I think you feel unseen, unappreciated, rejected, shit on, etc. The list goes on. And because you carry that with you, you can't express it all the time. You have compensated a life over it and that is what keeps you from functioning organically. Also, a lot of your tensions and your re-entry into the acting field is complicated by this feeling. We have to— you say deprogramming, and I'll use another word— expurgation. Getting rid of all those feelings. Looking at them very rationally and very logically. Let me ask you a question. In this room do you feel any of those feelings that I suggested? Being unseen, misunderstood, unappreciated, any or all of those feelings?

C: No, I don't feel it in this room. I used to.

E: You don't feel it in this room? Do you feel that we accept you and understand you?

C: Yeah, I really do.

E: Then where do you feel it?

C: I'm not feeling it as much anymore. I was feeling it, really feeling it. I feel so much more support now and a lot of love from a lot of people.

E: Okay. You know what else you're feeling? More than a little love. You feel sorry for yourself. More than a little bit.

C: No!

E: That's okay. I feel that you do. And that energy could be used in a much more productive way. How many years did you spend being involved in the war?

C: Five years.

E: Do you feel a loss of those five years?

C: I feel a complete loss since 1966.

E: Fourteen years, that's a long time.

C: I can't remember a lot of what happened. I've blocked out many things.

E: That's a long time. Do you feel also that you've blown a lot of time?

C: Yeah.

E: Do you feel like it's not replaceable?

C: No, I just look back and ask, "What happened to those years? What did I do with them? Where have I been? What have I done?" I've been on some kind of cloud. Been very nebulous, haven't been feeling anything. That's why I get so frightened in here sometimes, feeling so much the pain and the intensity, because I haven't felt love or anything. I haven't been even giving love to anybody, much less receiving it. I just totally closed myself off.

E: I want you to get these feelings of resentment and anger out. Put them out, because what it does is makes you feel like a martyr. It makes you feel sorry for yourself, and it makes you alienate yourself, back off from people, on a very subtle level if not on a very obvious level. In class, in this work you have to eliminate those things because they are of significant obstacles in terms of functioning.

C: How do you mean that? I don't think I quite know what you mean.

E: Well, the first part is to become aware that you're doing it. You're holding all these resentments and feelings and it puts you apart from people and it serves no good purpose. You should express your feelings and look at them for what they really are. Do I really feel that much hurt or am I adding to this? I think there's another element there that's really important. I get the feeling from you that it's not so much that you put yourself out, you really feel those things and you really want to do those things, but you don't take good care of yourself in doing them. Emotionally, take care of yourself. You can put yourself out, get involved in what you feel strongly about, give to the people but you've gotta make sure that when you feel strongly you can handle it, that nobody is shitting on you, that you are getting back what you are putting out. You have to take care of yourself. I think for you it's very important to be very, very conscious of "Am I taking care of myself?" Watch out for yourself.

A Dream

"Dear God, thank you for the day," but I couldn't pray.

In the middle of the night, I found myself screaming at this huge, black, bird-monster hovering over my head, devouring me—a combination of bird and human. "Don't kill me!" I screamed, terrified by its horrifying screech.

Many times in New York, I didn't even want to leave my apartment, but forced myself to go out.

I told the psychiatrist my husband had died, and that I really needed help. He looked at me and said: "I don't think you need me. I don't think I can help you."

"What do you mean I don't need a psychiatrist. Can't you see that I'm unhappy. Can't you see I'm miserable?" I asked, sobbing. "Why do you think I came to see you? Why do you think I paid you all this money? What do you mean I'm not crazy? Look at me, look at me!"

When he recommended that I see a woman psychiatrist, I went to see David Yarosh instead. He was always happy and full of smiles. During my stay in New York, David turned out to be the only thing I felt good about. He was a friend I could talk to.

Why can't I say, "God bless you"? Why doesn't it feel good? In moments of total horror when life was going out of a GI, why could I only look at him feeling numb?

I remember seeing one guy; I went over and said, "Hi." He lay there staring straight ahead without blinking, without saying anything— shell-shocked, gone! His body was there, his mind somewhere else. That's how I feel about myself— paralyzed.

Dreams can be so frightening that it is a wonder I haven't died from fright. In February 1982, the National Center for Disease Control in Atlanta, Georgia, on investigating the death of eighteen Laotian refugees in different parts of the United States, found they had all died in the middle of the night as a result of what many now call the nightmare death syndrome.

I've spent my life trying to win the admiration of people instead of directing my life toward God. Yes, I followed the Golden Rule and the Ten Commandments, but frequently slipped, as in a Florence Nightingale letter:

"I see so many of my kind who have gone mad for want of something to do. Mad and subject to outbursts. When night comes, women suffer— even physically. The accumulation of nervous energy, which has nothing to do during the day, makes them feel every night, when they go to bed as if they were going mad."

Is that what's happening to me? Have I turned on myself, hating myself, despising my weaknesses?

I prayed to God morning and night to help me, to save me, to show me the way. I was told to pray to the Son to reach the Father. As most of my friends in show business were Jewish, I didn't think a whole lot about Jesus.

I began reading all kinds of metaphysical books. Realizing I hadn't the faintest idea what all those intellectuals and popular authors were talking about, I threw them across the room.

I had been looking for something to interest me, but nothing did. I wished I were more spiritual so that I could better grasp and search for peace with myself and God. What was this fight going on inside of me?

The headaches were so bad I went to see a nutritionist who asked me if I was angry. I quickly replied, "No, maybe once in a while, when a car pulls in front of me. No, I'm seldom angry." That question preyed on my mind and I realized that I was very angry, but didn't fully comprehend what I was angry about. I just couldn't believe that the war and its effects could continue to disturb me.

Black Veterans

"I . . . do solemnly swear that I will bear true faith and allegiance to the United States of America; that I will serve them honestly and faithfully against all their enemies whosoever; and that I will obey the orders of the President of the United States and the orders of the officers appointed over me according to regulations and the Uniform Code of Military Justice."

In 1965, Malcolm X urged black men not to fight Uncle Sam's wars, but to fight for black liberation.

Black brothers loved it when I played, *Say it Loud, I'm Black, I'm Proud,* by James Brown. They threw their fists in the air, to the dismay of the white commanders. However, it encouraged them to go out in the field to fight and be outstanding soldiers. Notwithstanding the racial issues, black and white soldiers fought together in saving each other's lives.

One black brother told me, "You were ok; we never thought of you as that white bitch."

"I was firing from a gunship to the music of *Magic Carpet Ride*", another told me. "We were right outside of Pleiku and not one American got hurt that night."

Another said, "I was in LBJ, (Long Binh Jail). In order to go to the latrine we had to raise our hand and the guard would let one or two go out at a time. I was just sitting there listening to *Cloud Nine* on the guard's radio."

A white Special Forces Green Beret brother, John Gallagher, from Brooklyn, New York, was captured along with the rest of his team. Since it was the first entire A team captured by the VC, the enemy wanted to use them as an example. The VC kept the seven white men, one Indian, one black man, and three Latins in separate eight-foot holes. They had to go to the bathroom, fight off the rats, and sleep in the mud from the rain in a hole that didn't even have enough room for them to lie down. Through the steel lid that covered his hole, John Gallagher could hear the VC's radio. John told me later, "Everyday your voice would come on the radio, and I could hear the music. How bizarre to hear a *round-eyed* American woman's voice on a VC radio inside Cambodia! You made us realize we still had a chance of making it out alive." When I asked him why, he said, "Because we knew Americans were still there and weren't going to forget about us. We knew they would do something; we knew that we weren't forgotten. Just hearing your voice gave us hope. The biggest thing is you still made us feel a part of home. Knowing that made us want to stay alive. I heard that sexy voice and knew that one day I had to meet this woman. Once a day, for one hundred and forty-four days, we were pulled up by a rope for our only meal of rice, water, maggots, roaches and rat meat. We ate it to survive. Those of us who were weak and didn't have the strength to hold on to the rope were tied to the rope by a VC who jumped into the hole. We had never seen you, but we dreamed of you as blonde and blue-eyed until the day seven of us escaped."

Moon Child
  I have read rather extensively about those living under
the sign of Cancer. I am a Cancer, a moon child, having
been born July 2nd.
  In my very early years there was discord and tension in
my family life. My father left when I was very young.
Fortunately, my mother remarried a very fine man, David
Botz. He took on the role of our real father, working hard to
support us.
  In spite of that support, I felt insecure. In Cancer, or
Moon children, "still water runs deep." Win or lose, I
seldom showed my feelings. When I lost, I rationalized by
saying that I tried hard and that there would always be the
next time.
  A Cancer is tenacious, conscientious, earnest and thor-
ough. Yes, that's me— emotionally rich, always well-or-
ganized, stable, steady, and money-oriented. At sixteen I
had several odd jobs to pay for personal things. At seventeen, I moved to New York looking for work— and that
may make me also courageous. However, I don't know
what to make of all those Cancer attributes.
  Moon children are clever and calculating, though money
never meant that much in my younger years, because there
were always ways to earn material things. I craved a home
of my own. I craved happiness and a family. I did have
beautiful homes which I decorated. Did I achieve happiness? No! Did I get a family of my own? No! To think that
many men and women have all of that and throw it away!
For what?

13
Without Forethought

"We prepared our men for war in Vietnam, not for their return to this country", contends Shad Meshad, who has counseled thousands of veterans in the past 15 years in his position as the creator and pioneer of the VA Operation Outreach program. His helicopter was shot down, its blades scalping him. He had to use a bandana to hold up his face. A psychiatric officer on the battle field, back home, he had no less readjustment problems than other veterans, many of whom have been in and out of medical and psychiatric hospitals since their release from active duty. They suffer flashbacks, nightmares, anger and deep, deep depression—typical PTSD (Post Traumatic Stress Disorder). Many live in remote areas. Others, if they don't commit suicide, they think about it on a regular basis.

Tom Williams, a psychologist and consultant for the Disabled American Veterans, has clinically treated hundreds of veterans. "If a guy comes to see me," he observed, "and says he has never thought of suicide, I know he's lying. Vets have a background of violence and killing—that's what separates them from the regular population. They are more prone to act it out."

I can attest to hundreds and hundreds of these veterans who have told me about their thoughts, their suicide trends, their deep depressions and irritations with their loved ones. Knowing that the nation has let them down has simply exacerbated their PTSD.

The Walking Wounded

They were simply placed on a plane and flown back. No reception, little love, just hate and ridicule. Then one wonders why so many Vietnam veterans are in jails. Many are found dead, like Jim Hopkins with a bottle of alcohol next to him and some pills, or another found dead on a railroad track. And those one-man car accidents off sides of roads. While driving, I felt those moments of rage: "Ah, to hell with it all!" (Thank God I knew better). It's so easy, so fast! Why continue? No one to talk to. I call them the *walking wounded*, or *Trip Wire Vets*. There are Vietnam veterans living in caves and off the land, who, refusing to deal with a thankless, egotistical, and materialistic society, just walk and walk and walk.

While at an outdoor restaurant with Craig Wyckoff, my agent, this guy walked up and asked for some change. When I didn't respond, he walked away to another table. I said, "He's a Vietnam veteran." Craig was about to ask me how I knew, when the veteran began to talk to these two young guys at the next table. "Man, all I want from you is some change for something to eat. That's all I ask for," he said, pausing for a few seconds, then continued in an angry tone, "F . . . it. I fought in the f . . . war and nobody gives a shit. Nobody cares. You probably weren't even there."

"Wait a minute," I said as he was passing by. I looked deep into his eyes full of anger. "Were you in Vietnam?"

"Why! Were *you* in Vietnam?" he asked, expecting a negative answer.

"Yes," I answered matter of fact. Stunned, he reverted to a little boy. "Who were you with?" I asked.

"The 101st," he said, pulling his sleeve to show a big tattoo of the 101st Airborne.

"I know the 101st. Look," I added, "I won't give you any money, but I'm going to give you the name of a place to go if you ever want to talk to someone about what's going on with you. I want you to have this." I handed him a card from the Vet Center, and a quarter for the phone call. He just looked at it, turned around, said a simple thank you and walked away. From where I was sitting, I could see him walk across the street, down past another street and continued walking as far as I could see him.

He stopped trying to get money and food because I had broken his train of thought by acknowledging the fact he had been in Vietnam. Had anyone asked if he had been in Vietnam and said, "It's okay!" instead of, "You were in Vietnam, you stupid asshole," things might have been different.

I was happy to see Craig notice how that man had changed as a result of a few positive words. Just before I spoke to him, he was looking at these two young guys, remembering himself when he was their age and thinking how easy those guys had it. At that moment, I realized one very important thing: their survival meant my survival as well, and that of the thousands of suffering veterans.

Those eyes! I recognized the look in his eyes, the look I would soon see everywhere I went throughout America.

Women Veterans
In Hollywood I tried to get back in the movie business. I did commercials and small parts in TV movies, nothing to brag about. I was too shaky and had those constant head-aches. A friend suggested my contacting Lynda Van Devanter, a nurse who had been in Vietnam. I hesitated because I didn't want to recount the same old stories and get upset. I saw a few Red Cross women and nurses, and wondered if they had the same problems. I didn't really think this woman and I would have anything   in common, and felt stupid and shy in calling her.

When I finally called her, she greeted me with a pleasant, "Hi Chris, how are you?" She sounded as though we had known each other for ages. On my way to see her, I questioned why I was going, thinking I needed this like a hole in the head. Almost turning back several times, I was late and worked myself into a frenzy.

She changed all that by being friendly. As we talked, I felt the presence of an understanding family member, a sister—Vietnam sisters who had faced the same reactions here and abroad.

On arriving in Vietnam, her idealistic view of the war, like mine, quickly vanished. Working long and arduous hours in cramped and ill-equipped, understaffed operating rooms, seeing friends die, witnessing a war close-up, operating on soldiers and civilians whose injuries were catastrophic, she found the very foundations of her thinking changing daily. After one traumatic year, she returned home, a Vietnam veteran. But coming home was nearly as devastating as going to Vietnam.

I realized that other women who had experienced Vietnam had a lot in common with me.

She encouraged me to read books, but I told her I preferred movies over books because at the movies I wouldn't be alone. With a book by myself, I'd freak out.

After she left, I sat in my car for a while. Deciding to take her advice, I drove to a local book store. On asking the clerk about books on Vietnam, another patron who overheard me turned around and said, "Why do you want a book about Vietnam?" After telling me to go f . . . myself, he rushed out of the store. And this could still happen in the 80's!

On seeing *Coming Home* with my sister Trudie, I got upset when the officer, back from Vietnam, walked into the ocean and killed himself. "Oh, I'm fine; it doesn't bother me. I'm okay," I said to reassure Trudie when she saw me frowning. But I wasn't "okay". It bothered me a lot because all I could think of was Ty killing himself. I was still denying my feelings to others.

Because of a new awareness of other women's experiences, I began to feel I was not alone anymore, and that I wasn't going crazy after all.

Martha Raye was the only other woman I knew who had been in Vietnam. Maggie didn't talk much about Vietnam.

One night though, Maggie sat down on the floor and started crying— crying about a major she had loved in Vietnam and who had died on the battle field. She cried and cried.

I remember seeing her on the floor, crying and mumbling about how much she'd loved that man, how it hurt to see him lying dead. At that moment, I did not really understand her grief as I hadn't yet dealt with those problems. She looked so frail on that floor, and so small.

On stage she sang, *Going Out Of My Head*, the best I had ever heard. Oh, Maggie, How I respect your strength and courage!

Lynda Van Devanter and I went to see *Tracers*, a play by and about seven veterans playing GIs. We sat in the first row, practically paralyzed. In one scene, they re-enacted the "blanket party"— going around collecting bits and pieces of bodies and wrapping them up in a blanket. Lynda and I reached, grabbed each other's hand, and held on tight. After it was over, she cried on the director's shoulders and I had to grasp the chair to remind myself that I was in a theater. I thought I was going to explode.

"Chris!" one of the actors yelled. "Chris Noel? Wow! I used to listen to you on the radio. Wow!" More of them came over and told me how happy they were to meet me—the bond was obvious. I couldn't believe they remembered me.

While working on Vietnam Veterans activist rallies, guys would come up and say, "Chris Noel! God, I used to listen to you all the time." Others would look, turn around, and walk away. Then they would come back to tell me that meeting me was very hard— I brought back memories they were trying to forget.

When I was in New York, I needed a copy of a photograph of me in Vietnam. When I went back to pick up the pictures, the clerk at the photo store kept staring at me. I didn't think much about it since New York City has all kinds of strange people. On giving me my change, he mumbled something like, "Thank you for saving my friend's life."

"What friend?" I asked in amazement.

"My very best friend was in Vietnam. When he came back, all he talked about was you. I didn't know who you were, but all he talked about was how if it weren't for you and your radio show and being able to listen to your voice, he would've killed himself."

"Where's your friend now?"

"Nobody knows. He came back from Vietnam. He was here for two weeks, and he just disappeared. Nobody's seen him since—not his family, not his friends. It's been years."

One veteran recently said to me, "I need you and you need us. You keep me alive! These vets in the wheelchairs keep me alive! We need each other! And, don't you ever forget it!"

I have encounters like these all the time. This encourages me to work harder on behalf of our Vietnam veterans.

"Ladies and gentlemen, I'm about to do the impossible," said the circus announcer in a Marilyn Monroe movie. It struck me so much that I wrote it down in my notebook.

Ladies and gentlemen, my veteran friends and I are doing the impossible!

14
Agent Orange

Another horror I have been harboring is the possible effects of Agent Orange on my physical system. Yes, I was exposed to it many times. We often landed by helicopter out in the boonies after Agent Orange had been sprayed. And, of course, I did drink water contaminated by that poison.

In my dreams, I see orange-striped 55-gallon drums, some empty, some full, on roadways and in the bushes, mists of spray not yet settled, orders coming and our men advancing through mists, charging forward.

A defoliant containing dioxin, Agent Orange has been known to be one of the most potent carcinogens in existence. Many veterans have died of cancer; others have found tumors in their heads and spines, others have had hip replacements, yet others got cases of *jungle rot*— fungus or liver spots on the skin.

It is a horror story of hundreds of veterans stricken with the dreaded diseases resulting from Agent Orange. Afflicted parents give birth to deformed offsprings. To have a fairly good idea about Agent Orange, one needs but to read, *Kerry, Agent Orange And An American Family* by Clifford Linedecker, or talk to the Krumpton family of four boys. The one born before Vietnam is healthy; the three born since Vietnam have brain damage. The family holds a yearly Children of Agent Orange Christmas party where I see so many brain-damaged children.

Agent Orange Victims International (AOVI) has been instrumental in exposing the illegal chemical dumping of toxic chemicals in America. Founded by Paul Reutershan, a combat Vietnam veteran, who realized the need to provide the special services necessary to help those affected, Paul, through his extensive media coverage, shocked the nation with these words: "I died in Vietnam and didn't know it." On December 14, 1978, he died of cancer at the age of 28. Since his death, courageous Vietnam veterans and their families have come together under the banner of AOVI to carry on Paul's vital work, led by Frank McCarthy and Jimmy Sparrow.

Rats and mice used in lab tests gave birth to dead offsprings or with cleft palates, with no eyes, with cystic kidneys and enlarged livers.

Humans have developed chloracne symptoms which include skin eruptions on the face, neck and back, shortness of breath, intolerance to cold, palpable and tender liver, loss of sensation in the extremities, damage to nerves, fatigue, nervousness, irritability, insomnia, loss of libido, and vertigo. In Hanoi there are hundreds of jars containing fetuses with six fingers and toes, one eye, no arms or legs, totally distorted.

From 1962 to 1971, everyone who was in the field of Vietnam was exposed to toxic herbicides which were also sprayed around base camp perimeters, landing zones, mine fields, fire bases, along roadways and river banks, carried out by truck, boat or backpack, by C-123 cargo planes and helicopters with their many aborted spray mission dumpings in so-called "free spray areas".

The military region most heavily sprayed was III Corps followed by I, II and IV Corps. In addition, unknown amounts of herbicide were sprayed by air. Some areas were sprayed with both herbicides and pesticides. Bathing or drinking water automatically exposed that individual to Agent Orange.

The reason Agent Orange symptoms have taken so long to surface is due to the slow effect rate and diverse symptomology: dioxins and other chlorinated hydrocarbons are stored in the body tissues and released at a later time, especially during weight loss. They don't seem to leave the body.

A class action suit filed by Vietnam veterans against Dow Chemical, Monsanto, Diamond/Shamrock, Uniroyal and Thompson/Hayward produced thousands of pages of documents proving these companies knew, since 1964, the extreme toxicity of the chemical. Warning words were written on labels: *usually not disabling, but may be fatal.* Yet dioxin is 70,000 times more potent than a drop of cyanide. An out-of-court settlement was made.

"I even thought of building a home in Vietnam."

Drinking with the GIs in the field.

Ty survived Vietnam—not America.

With General Westmoreland—trying to survive
America.

15
Me, A Feminist?

A prevalent neurosis among our veterans is anxiety. It becomes evident when thinking about or in the presence of danger. We live with this neurosis.

A lot of guys don't like being called "vets" because it makes them feel like animals. A guy said, "Vet Center! People think we're f . . . animals. Well, that's how they think about us anyway." Many even object to the granite memorial monument built in Washington for the Vietnam veterans, preferring the American flag and statue to the black granite slabs. Others cry as they touch the names of our dead.

On one Fourth of July, while staying in a very peaceful section of Long Island with a wonderful guy, Jerry Becker, I heard firecrackers. I knew what they were. When the first one went off, I just about jumped out of the bed. "The Fourth of July! Damn it, the firecrackers. Go back to sleep," I told myself. I kept flashing to Tet— to this big mask I had bought, that the Vietnamese used in their parades—this big, huge, colorful mask I wanted so badly.

My response embarrassed me, for I did not want Jerry to see me like this. I didn't want him to see how shaky I really was.

There I was, knowing it was firecrackers, telling myself it was nothing to be afraid of, even laughed about it, saying, "What's wrong with you? Stop this!" At the same time, however, I was saying, "What if Jerry finds out about this?"

Many veterans are neither married nor with a woman. If married, they're with their second or third wife. Too many women just did not wait for their men to come back. Seeing them reading their "Dear John" letters made me wonder about these women.

In 1986, people say, "We've got to help these men." Back then, it was, "How wrong the war was. F . . . the men." Then the cover-up: "We protested because we wanted to get our men out of Vietnam." That's not the way I remember it.

Hostages

One veteran locked up in a Louisiana jail requested that he be sentenced to death for killing a police officer, preferring death to life in prison. It happened at the time when the Americans were returning from Iran. He slit his wrists to protest the heroes' welcome given them. There were reports of similar attempts by other veterans. Though I was happy to have our hostages back— free at last!— I must admit being angry and confused over America's parades and celebrations with all the activities at the White House. How could America open its loving arms to one group and disparage the heroes who risked their lives and limbs? I spoke to Ron Kovic, a paralyzed veteran author of *Born on the Fourth of July*, about my thoughts, and held a press conference with a handful of veterans at Liberty Hall in Los Angeles. Within days, veterans across America stepped out of the closet: "What about us?"

A miracle started; the healing began to take place. Veterans talked about their feelings of neglect. To our surprise, America began to listen.

But, as it turned out, America only listened, thus forcing the veterans to begin to help one another, to continue the healing process with or without outside help.

We built our own granite Vietnam Veterans Memorial in Washington inscribed with over 58,000 names of those who died in Southeast Asia and gave it to the American people.

Reunions, stress clinics and memorial services were being held throughout the country.

Bet On A Vet!

In the late '70s, I got a call from a production company telling me it was producing a campaign for the Department of Labor aimed at Vietnam veterans, its slogan: "Bet on a Vet", the aim to inform them of their employment rights. Elated, I accepted though I didn't know what was expected of me. The only thing I knew was that aside from the expenses, there would be no pay, as usual.

I had just gotten a new Yorkshire Terrier. I took my little dog, and together with my *spiritual* friend, Frances Hillin, we went off to Pennsylvania.

After completing the camera work for *Bet On A Vet*, the campaign was suddenly called off. The Women's Division of the Department of Labor in Denver, Colorado, started a big protest. Claiming sexism, women began to tear down my posters. I guess they didn't like my pose— a simple head shot which, if it looked like anything, it resembled a typical Breck ad. Its caption read: " . . . Vietnam veterans, take advantage of your employment rights . . . Call your local Department of Labor office."

When I talked to the woman who wrote the first protest letter, I learned that I looked too good. I called the head of NOW (National Organization of Women) in LA. She said her group would absolutely not support me: "If any woman's group said it was sexism, it was sexism," she retorted, refusing to talk about it, or to look at the poster so she could better decide for herself. "You should not have done it in the first place," she added.

"Why?"

"Because you're a woman."

"What's that got to do with it?" I asked, my voice controlled.

"You're appealing to Vietnam veterans, and that means you're appealing to men. A woman shouldn't be involved in a campaign that appeals to men."
"I don't understand. I thought NOW encouraged women to achieve. I earned my right in Vietnam," I rebutted even if I sounded defensive.
"I'm sorry I can't help you," she answered flatly.
"You have helped me more than you can possibly imagine," I said curtly, and hung up.

Phyllis Schlafley
A few days later, I read in the paper that Phyllis Schlafley was against NOW and the ERA (Equal Rights Amendment). She felt ERA would destroy family life, promote homosexuality, expose women to the draft, and foster abortion.
"Chris," she said affably, "Can you come to Springfield tomorrow and hold a press conference at the capitol?"
"Yes," I answered without hesitation.
I got on a plane for Springfield only to find I was heading for the wrong Springfield— there are so many.
I've always been a woman who did what needed to be done. In spite of being female and pretty I took chances. When one has these attributes, a woman really has to fight her way because some people think she's dumb, particularly if blonde, as I am.
Phyllis explained that the women's groups did not want the ten-point preference given to veterans on the civil-service exams. So, it was the women's groups against the veterans, and there I was in the middle of it all.
I spent the evening with Phyllis and her family. I was amazed to see how they worked to support her. At the dinner table, we talked about politics from beginning to end— her husband and kids included: no childish stuff, everyone an adult! I had never sat in a family unit like that. This woman, who is being condemned by so many women, has put it all together. I would love to have a family with kids like hers.
Sometime later, when I was in Los Angeles, I wrote her a letter asking her, if she ever came to California, to have

dinner with me. A few days later, I was invited to a dinner party being attended by Phyllis. On walking in, I was offered a fruit cocktail with whipped cream. No alcohol! I was impressed by those present: writers, scientists, actors, directors, businessmen, etc.

Sitting next to Phyllis, I started to talk about our veterans, about Delayed Stress and Agent Orange. As I was talking, I noticed from across the table a gentleman listening attentively. He was a World War II veteran. All of a sudden, he began to crack jokes apparently directed at me.

A movie director, who had been in the Korean War, couldn't understand what was so special about Vietnam veterans. When I tried to explain about Delayed Stress, he got upset, bringing the entire room to silence. Tension was evident. Phyllis took over and put an end to it.

Gretchen Wyler, who heads the LA Humane Society, was sitting next to me. "You think this is a bitch. Imagine what it was like for me being in the dining room doing all the work I do on behalf of animals, while they were sitting at dinner talking about hunting trips and stuffed game animals they have at home," she whispered. Nudging me, she continued: "Don't give in. You're doing great!"

Maureen Reagan
Following excerpt is from the *Maureen Reagan Radio Show* February 7, 1981: (MMaureen, CChris)

M: Last week for those who were with us, you will remember that we were discussing how people felt. Although everyone was joyous at the return of the hostages from Iran, the juxtaposition of that to the treatment of the returning Vietnam veterans was the opposite. In the course of that, a woman called and was upset because she is a woman veteran of the Vietnam War and couldn't find any place for women with problems to go for help. So we thought it might be a good idea to follow up on that discussion this week, and find out what programs were available for women. So we invited an old friend into the studio. Her name is Chris Noel; she is a fantastic actress, but doesn't do

it anymore. She used to be with Armed Forces Radio . . .
I'm awful glad you're with us . . .
C: Thank you. I'm happy to be here.
M: . . . When you discovered . . . we're talking about
not only the prolonged effect of Vietnam and our attitude
toward those who returned, but also people who weren't
necessarily veterans as such but even more important women who served in Vietnam, we don't know how many
there are that just haven't had anybody to talk to. When
you realized that you were suffering this delayed shock,
this reaction that we now know is much more common
than we thought five or ten years ago, where did you go?
C: I sought help with a therapist on a one-to-one basis
and also in group . . . I discovered the Vet Centers Outreach Program . . .
M: Let's talk about the program. What does the Vet
Center do for somebody?
C: Primarily rap groups. One of the big problems the
veterans have faced is the alienation from their friends and
families . . . They help in securing jobs and housing. The
rap groups are very important as they allow venting their
thoughts and feelings . . .
W: (Woman veteran on the phone) So many women
who returned were looking for someplace to find compan-
ionship, and some people who had shared the same kinds
of experiences found it impossible to do so because the
traditional organizations wouldn't admit us . . .
L: (Listener on the phone) . . . I think the Vietnam vets
should know that what they did was right . . . that what
they did was absolutely in the best interest not only for the
country but for humanity. Any further questions as to the
systems of government, let them look at the *Gulag*. Let
them see . . . how many people have been killed. Let them
look at people like Lillian Helman, who spent her life de-
fending Stalinism that killed so many millions of people
. . .
C: . . . Right, this is obviously a very emotional subject
for everyone. Those who served in Vietnam, those who
stayed home watching it on their TV or those who didn't
watch it on TV, it's been said there is nothing that can be

done about it. There is something that can be done about it, now and for the future. Many men and women went to Vietnam because they loved America. Their country asked them to do it. The taxpaying citizens are as much responsible as the men and women who were in Vietnam. I think it's time that America started loving and remembering the forgotten warriors . . .

V: (Veteran on the phone) . . . I think that essentially the country needs to review that whole Vietnam experience which has been the most fundamental happening in our country in the last 25 years. I think that those psychologically traumatic effects from the Vietnam War will continue to be felt by millions of people in our country . . .

M: Okay. Now my next question is going to be . . . We have done an incredible job of welcoming home the Iranian hostages . . .

Hunger Strike

Wearing fatigues, Jim Hopkins drove his red vintage Jeep up the long walkway leading to the Wadsworth VA Hospital where he had been an outpatient. Turning his jeep around, he backed through two sets of glass doors, showered glass on himself, and after ordering the people to get out of the lobby, he began to fire his weapons. After his arrest, he was held for psychiatric evaluation and eventually released.

Pursuant to the incident, he told me that he never meant to harm anyone, that he was happy and proud to have served his country and would do it again. I felt he definitely needed help, especially when he told me that to feel better, he would dress in camouflage, go to the hills, and practice reconnaissance. Days later, he was found dead—apparent suicide. By the side of his bed were alcohol and pills.

To the Los Angeles veterans, he was a hero. Jim's dramatized plea for medical help was so dramatic that the veterans hoped it would force the VA to re-examine its treatment policies.

The upshot is that when the Los Angeles hunger strike of Vietnam veterans happened, I was packing my suitcase to visit my family in Florida when I got a call from Morton Blackwell, public liaison with veterans groups to President Reagan.

"Chris Noel, this is Morton Blackwell. My wife is Phyllis Schlafley's executive secretary. We know that there are Vietnam veterans in Los Angeles right now on a hunger strike and my wife tells me that Phyllis said that you were the person we should talk to. We need some help. Would you please go and find out what the hunger strikers want?"

"I know what they want. They're my friends. I bought the tents and the sleeping bags for them. What else do you want to know?"

"We want to know exactly what they want. This isn't a good thing to be happening in our country. Vietnam veterans shouldn't have to be on a hunger strike to get what they need."

I hung up the phone. I was dumbfounded! I had just received a call from President Reagan's special advisor on Veterans Affairs. Without wasting time I went to see the guys to ask them what they wanted. Scotty and Marlin, their leaders, immediately wrote it down in their own handwriting. I called the White House and read the list. Blackwell called back.

"Chris, we're writing a document that we're going to send out to the hunger strikers and we think that everybody's going to be very pleased with it. There's some wonderful things in it and it really states how the President feels."

After several conversations back and forth well into the night, I finally got a local call: "They're all leaving the hunger strike; they're getting out of there to get some sleep."

The media was there with its photographers. We're not talking about guys giving up food for more than two weeks who were formerly healthy. These strikers were already in hospitals, sick to begin with, who shouldn't have been on hunger strikes. Some were getting blood in their stools.

The protesters were now divided into two groups: one inside the lobby of the Wadsworth VA Hospital, and the hunger strikers outside.

"We'd been on this strike for ten days," they said, "before you guys decided to go inside the hospital to protest. We stopped eating because we hadn't seen a doctor in weeks. All we were given were pills every day and nobody would talk to us and nothing was happening and we weren't getting well. So we just stopped eating. Might as well not even eat. We'll just die of not eating."

Lots of people showed up including bikers and hippy freaks. One man, with long grey hair and long beard, bouncing up and down for hours like a pogo stick. His picture was in the paper with a caption, "He's a Vietnam veteran." The man didn't even know where Vietnam was. He just stood in front of the Federal Building, holding signs pushing to legalize marijuana.

"Listen," I said to him, "you can really hurt the veterans by constantly telling people the whole world should be smoking pot. A lot of guys are trying to get off drugs," I observed. When veterans spoke up, he put his marijuana signs away and pretended to be a Vietnam veteran.

Morton Blackwell called me back and said, "Got senior staff approval. Only one problem. The head of the Veterans Administration just resigned. We have to wait for President Reagan to appoint someone else. It's between two men right now." In a another call, he said, "Chris, we got it, we got it! The President has just sworn in Dr. Donald Custis as the acting administrator and this is what's in the document. We're going to send a copy. It has Custis' signature on it, but I'm guaranteeing you that everything in that document comes from the President himself, personally."

"The President has asked me to inform you . . . ," I said. I took down the different points and gave them to the strikers. They all came upstairs to the hospital administrator's office. Satisfied with the document, we called a press conference which angered two of the organizers— Ron Kovic and Ron Bitzer, who felt we should not have had it without them, but the whole thing was so sudden. I read the points to the press in the presence of a lot of excited veterans. It was the first time a President had made a personal commitment to keep the Vet Centers open for three years, with double funding for the centers for 26 million dollars. Everyone agreed that President Reagan was an honorable man, that once he knew about their problems, he would do what was right. Dane, another veteran, said he did not believe in the American system. Now that he saw what a handful of veterans could do, he was elated.

All of a sudden, a group of angry veterans came up to us. I didn't even know which ones were actually veterans. They demanded that we not talk to the press without talking to them. "The hunger strike isn't over," someone yelled, "We want to speak to President Reagan personally!"

When a couple of guys began lashing at me, I said, "As far as the original hunger strikers are concerned, their portion of the strike is over. If you want to start one, that's up to you."

I knew I had one loyal supporter. He put a big sign on his tent which said, "Vietnam Veterans Love Chris Noel." I never saw that sign, however. I was tired and went home to Florida for a rest.

16

Traitor!

"*T* reason against the United States shall consist only in levying war against them, or to adhering to their enemies, giving them aid and comfort." (Article 3, Section 3, United States Constitution)

Treason: betrayal, treachery, or breach of allegiance or of obedience toward the sovereign or government. (Funk and Wagnalls Dictionary)
   The treason clause in the US Constitution was defined by our American Founding Fathers.

Axis Sally
   Mildred Gillars, better known as Axis Sally, was a native of Maine, an unsuccessful actress, and a student of music in France. In 1940, she became a disc jockey for Radio Berlin. In 1944, weeks before D-Day, she recorded a radio drama, *Vision of an Invasion*. In this drama, in which one heard blood curdling cries and shrieking voices of sobbing GIs, she was acting out what would happen to American soldiers if they invaded Nazi-held territories. On other shows, between records, she made comments like, "Damn

Roosevelt," "Damn Churchill," "Damn all the Jews who have made this war possible."

"I love America," she would say, "but I don't love Roosevelt and his *Kike* boyfriends." She became the object of hate among the US military and former POWs, and was arrested at the end of the war.

Axis Sally would visit the prisoner-of-war camps in Holland, France and Germany, on the pretense that she was a member of the Red Cross, and make tape recordings of their messages to their families in America. She promised she was not associated with any propaganda organization, but her broadcasts contained propaganda from beginning to end.

In the courtroom, one former POW recognized her and shouted, "She threatened us . . . that American citizen, that woman right there."

Another former POW said she screamed abuse when he wouldn't say favorable things about life in the prisoner-of-war camps.

A third former POW quoted her as saying, "You'll regret this." He had also refused to say what she demanded, as he suspected her to be a German government agent. Days later, he was sent to a concentration camp.

On March 11, 1948, *The New York Times* reported on the verdict: "The case against Miss Gillars seemed complete. She has admitted making wartime broadcasts for the Nazis, in the course of which she did what she could to break the morale of American soldiers on the firing lines and of their relatives at home. If she had been successful the war would have lasted longer and more men would have died. It was a dirty business . . . It is a story one would like to forget. But in returning this case to oblivion let us not minimize the crime of treason, which may cost lives, and more."

Axis Sally was sentenced to a ten to thirty years prison term. In 1985 she was living in Columbus, Ohio.

Tokyo Rose

Iva Ikuko Toguri, better known as Tokyo Rose, was born July 4, 1916 in Los Angeles and was educated at Compton

Junior College, then transferred to UCLA to study zoology.

On July 1, 1941, she went on a visit to Japan. With the bombing of Pearl Harbor, Iva was unable to return to America. To earn a living, she got a job with a broadcasting studio. As the war progressed, she continued to broadcast programs directed at making our GIs homesick. On March 1, 1943, she aired the famous *Zero Hour.*

Shortly after VJ Day, Iva was rounded up and eventually tried. After a long and extensive trial, covered internationally by the World Press, and known as the *Tokyo Rose Trial,* Iva was found guilty and sentenced to 10 years imprisonment and fined $10,000. Immediately, she was transported to a federal prison where she served six years and two months, before she received a full pardon from President Ford, the day before he left office.

During World War II, seven of twelve persons involved in propaganda radio broadcasts on behalf of the enemy were indicted for treason. Two were women: Mildred and Iva.

Hanoi Hannah

Hanoi Hannah went on the air from North Vietnam in September, 1964, with her daily half-hour English programs aimed at American GIs, especially black GIs, telling them they should be fighting their own war back home instead of in Vietnam. There were several women nicknamed Hanoi Hannah by our GIs on Radio Hanoi. They played American music (some programs were recorded in the U.S.) and said things to undermine the spirit of our fighting men: "Hi ya, GIs. How's everything with you fellows out there in the jungle tonight? Are the leeches climbing in and out of your uniform? Are the mosquitos chewing you to pieces? Are you trembling in fear over having to face the brave North Vietnamese in battle tonight or tomorrow? There is a simple way and quick way out of your unpleasant situation. And believe me, when I tell you this: surrender to the nearest North Vietnam Army unit and you will be well-treated and well-cared for by our great communist government of Hanoi. And I will also tell you

Ho Chi Minh sends you his warmest greetings and admires the brave American fighting men, but implores you to end the ceaseless struggle and surrender." Then she read her daily body count, the names of American boys killed in action. What a surprise for our guys to hear their own names read.

Hanoi Jane

Suddenly, the shock! An American woman read the following: "I beg you to consider what you are doing . . . All of you in the cockpits of your planes, on the aircraft carriers, those who are loading the bombs, those who are repairing the planes, those who are working on the Seventh Fleet, please think what you are doing. Are these people your enemies? What will you say to your children years from now who may ask you why you fought the war? What words will you be able to say to them?"

In a subsequent broadcast, the same voice announced: "The men who are ordering you to use these weapons are war criminals according to international law and in the past, in Germany and Japan, men who were guilty of these kinds of crimes were tried and executed. Why do you follow orders telling you to destroy a hospital or bomb the schools?"

And on another broadcast: "Tonight, when you are alone, ask yourselves: What are you doing? Accept no ready answers fed to you by rote from basic training on up. But as men, as human beings, can you justify what you are doing? Do you know why you are flying these missions? The people beneath your bombs have done us no harm."

The same voice also addressed the Vietnamese people: "We have understood that we have a common enemy— US imperialism . . . In our country people are very unhappy. People have no reason for living. They are very alienated from their work, from each other, and from history and culture . . . We hope very soon that, working together, we can remove the American cancer from your country so that the misery and unhappiness that has come to the American people very deep in their souls will not happen to the Vietnamese people."

Jane Fonda did not stop there: "POWs are lying if they assert it was the North Vietnamese policy to torture American prisoners."

She called on American servicemen to lay down their arms, and denounced the United States. She visited camps and posed with American POWs. To avoid posing or meeting with this American visitor, one POW took his small stool and beat on his face with it until it was red with blood.

At Michigan State University, she said to about 2000 students: "If you understood what communism was, you would hope, you would pray on your knees, that we would someday become communist."

At Duke University, she said: "I am a socialist, therefore I think we should strive toward a socialist society, all the way to communism. I would think that you would hope and pray on your knees that we would someday become communist."

In 1984, *Vogue* quoted her as saying: "Being the fourth most admired woman surprised me— sandwiched between Nancy Reagan and Mrs. Thatcher."

In Hollywood, she's led the way for successful actresses to produce their own films; in publishing, she's simply a phenomenon: sales of 1.25 million hardcover copies of *Jane Fonda's Workout Book* at $19.95, two years straight on the best-seller list; and her *Workout* video tape, the most successful ever made; and the *Workout* record with two million sold. In addition, she has highly profitable books and tapes for pregnant women, a 1984 Jane Fonda calendar that features health-food recipes, work-out clothes, a book for older women, and a tougher *Workout* tape called "Challenge."

The millions generated by these endeavours go to C.E.D. (Campaign for Economic Democracy). In November 1982, Jane's husband, activist and writer Tom Hayden, was elected to the California State Assembly in a campaign that ran up bills of nearly two million dollars. Fonda has contributed several million dollars to CED, making it one of the richest political organizations in California.

It amazes me to see women admire and support her endeavors as they do!

Frank McCarthy, pointman and tunnelrat for *The Big Red One*, is now President of Agent Orange Victims International: "The hypocrisy of all the anti-war leaders exists within the Agent Orange issue. During the war they all said that they were fighting to stop American boys from dying in Vietnam. Yet, when the war ended and Agent Orange emerged, those anti-war leaders like Jane Fonda, who made millions from the war, wouldn't donate one dime to our organization *Suicide Hot-Line* or *Medical Self-Help Guide*. Fonda, as well as all of the other anti-war leaders, knows that for Agent Orange victims the war never ended, that they are still dying from it and politics are all that Fonda will contribute."

Earl Hopper, retired Army Colonel, served as Chairman of the Board of the National League of Families of American Prisoners and Missing in Southeast Asia, and a leader of Task Force Omega: "There can be no doubt that Jane Fonda was a Communist Vietnamese sympathizer during the war. This was demonstrated by her perfidious acts both in Vietnam and here in the U.S. Her slanderous remarks about the American POWs are unforgivable. I am surprised she has survived so long."

(Some of the above information and all the following quotes and excerpts were taken from *The National Vietnam Veterans Review* article by Tom Carhart— November 1982, with permission by Chuck Allen, Editor.)

Chuck Allen, commander of Project Delta for Special Forces, said: "Jane Fonda was exploited as a propaganda tool by the North Vietnamese. She amused her peers, embarrassed her family, frustrated the State Department and enraged the American fighting man. She still disgusts me."

Jim Stockdale, retired vice admiral who was senior POW in his camp for four years, remembers Jane's visit well: "Only a picked few were ever shown to her— the other 98% of us only heard her recorded voice. We were committed to staying in prison until the North Vietnamese gave up, and we saw her as delaying those B-52 strikes which ultimately brought that about. In the eyes of most of us, she was killing Americans by lengthening the war."

Leo Thorseness, retired Air Force Colonel, was a POW for over six years: "Jane Fonda is an American embarrassment. In time of war, she went to North Vietnam, where she spit on the United States, posed for pictures in an antiaircraft gun that was used to shoot down US aircrafts, made propaganda broadcasts to our troops, and then came back to the US and laughed in our national face about it. I believe she was a traitor, and I don't understand why she was never formally charged with treason."

Larry DeMeo, company commander with the 173rd Airborne Brigade, works for the Veterans Administration: "Jane Fonda's real crime lies not so much in her undeniably treasonous activities, but rather in the fact that those activities encouraged the enemy to endure and so lengthened the war. Thousands of Americans and millions of Southeast Asians have died and are still dying as a result."

Jim Parker, rifleman with the 101st Airborne Division, is a columnist for the *Cleveland Plain Dealer:* "After my tour in Vietnam, I can remember times when I would gladly have killed her if I could have, but that blind rage has since cooled off, and now I simply have no time for her. There's no doubt in my mind that she committed treason, but I'm convinced she'll never be tried for it, and that bothers me. She certainly contributed to the suffering and deaths of many American soldiers, and in a society of laws, she should be punished, but, tragically, I'm afraid no one in a position of power in the government has the guts to go after her."

Howie Rutledge, retired Navy captain, has over six years as a POW: "Jane Fonda is an unfortunate anomaly—she has known nothing but comfort and wealth all her life, but denounces the American structures under which her family succeeded. It now seems that she has it both ways—she makes lots of money off 'the system', but she seems almost blindly driven to destroy that same system. I wouldn't be surprised by anything she might do to eliminate free enterprise in this country and replace it with her own ill-considered brand of socialism."

General Westmoreland, commander of all US forces in Vietnam for much of the war: "I believe it's rather disturbing that an individual so much in the public eye would have taken it upon herself to resist foreign policy that had been decided upon by elected officials . . . and it's really unconscionable that she would have made such a career out of undermining duly constituted authority. She had a very destructive effect on military morale, and it seemed she did everything she could to tear down pride of service to country and to turn enlisted men against their officers. Of course, she played a major role in the disillusionment that many Vietnam veterans later felt. I first thought that she was quite bright, but rather naive, and that she had simply been taken in by propaganda. Upon reflection, however, and in reviewing her long record of destructive opposition to the institutions of our society, I believe there is considerable evidence that she has been intentionally subversive and has been attempting to bring down the American system from within all along."

Dan Cragg, retired sergeant major, author of *The NCO Guide:* "A professional soldier can't afford to hold grudges against the people he is sworn to serve and defend, and that includes even Jane Fonda . . . but I am disappointed in her because she still refuses to admit that, when she visited North Vietnam, they weren't shooting horses, were they?"

Fred Smith, F-4 pilot with the Marine Corps, has established the Federal Express Company of which he is chairman of the board: "It's the end result that matters, and to the infantryman out there slogging around, trying to do his duty and still stay alive, the result of Jane Fonda's shrill theatrics on the world scene was just devastating as hell."

Jim Webb, platoon leader with the Marine Corps, author of *Fields of Fire* and *A Sense of Honor:* "Jane Fonda represents the gravest abuse of freedom in a democratic system. Her actions imply that individual opposition to government policy might permit direct collaboration with an enemy in its efforts to kill our citizens and destroy their morale. Hers was not a case of dissent, but rather one of treason."

Don Bailey, platoon leader with the 101st Airborne Division, served in Congress (D-PA): "Jane Fonda was wrong, but her aggressive attacks on those who served their country honorably will never be forgotten. She is the best-known of those foolish and befuddled Americans whose actions have resulted in the establishment of oppressive cruelty as deep and penetrating as any the world has ever known."

"Duncan Hunter, platoon leader with the 173rd Airborne Brigade, served in Congress (R-CA): "There is no doubt that Jane Fonda's alliance with the North Vietnamese Communists contributed to their military effort against American soldiers. Every mother, father, and loved one of Americans who were killed over there must decide for themselves what fault she should bear; I don't believe she will fare well when those personal and private judgments are made."

Tom Beasley, platoon leader with the First Cavalry Division, served as the director of the Republican Party in Tennessee: "What she did gave sustenance to the North Vietnamese and resulted in the deaths of many Americans. I believe she was a traitor, and I know she says she wasn't because Congress hadn't declared war, but when a guy in my platoon got killed by gunfire from a woodline, I didn't need an act of Congress to tell me who the enemy was."

Tom Pauken served as an adviser with MACV and is the Director of ACTION: "Jane and Tom and all their friends are the radical left wing and they'll use whatever works to bring our system down. Civil Rights, the Vietnam War, air pollution, nuclear power plants— if they think it will arouse great masses of people against the government. Of course, they are very insincere about what they say— look at Vietnam, where they were crying out against our heartless violence and then look at what they've done to protest the Communist blood bath that's been going on there since 1975— absolutely nothing. That ought to tell you a lot about them."

Murray McCann, rifleman with the Marine Corps, works for the US State Department: "Some people think she's a good actress, but that's beside the point. During the Vietnam War, I think she was a traitor. She got a lot of American soldiers killed by consorting with the enemy, and I don't think I'll ever forget that."

Tony Giufreda, rifleman with the Marine Corps, works for the Smithsonian Institute: "During the war, she was just a puppet and I don't know who was pulling her strings and I don't care. Since then, she's been jumping into negative causes: anti-nuke, anti-landlord, anti-this, anti-that— she thinks she's Joan of Arc, but I think she was nothing but a war profiteer with her movie *Coming Home*, making money and fame off of our blood and guts."

John Dramesi, retired Air Force colonel, escaped twice during his six years as a POW, is the author of *Code of Honor:* "Jane Fonda really caused a lot of difficulty for the whole country during the war. I'm not a lawyer, so I don't understand the technicalities, but I just can't believe that reasonable people wouldn't see her actions in Hanoi as treasonous. I have no interest in reopening old wounds, but I would think that just to assure the even application of our democratic system of laws, some formal examination and investigation of her actions in Hanoi should be made by the Federal Government."

John McCain is a retired Navy Captain in Arizona, and he also spent six years as a POW. "There is room in our society for all kinds of people. One of the great strengths of the United States is the allowance we give to peaceful disagreement by private citizens with governmental decisions— an allowance that simply doesn't exist in other countries. However, I believe that Jane Fonda exceeded her rights of citizenship when she went to Hanoi and provided aid and comfort to the enemy."

Fred Downs was a Platoon Leader with the 4th Infantry Division; he related his story in *The Killing Zone* (Norton, 1978). "Jane Fonda was one of the principal reasons that we, the men who fought the war, were seen by so many of our fellow Americans as genuinely bad people; that was hard to take then and it still is today."

Red McDaniel, six years a POW, retired Navy captain, is the author of *Scars and Stripes:* "When I was shot down in 1967, I was tortured regularly and methodically from the day I arrived in prison camp, and that happened to all the other prisoners with me. In 1969, for instance, the North Vietnamese found out about an escape attempt and kept me awake for seven days and seven nights, kneeling in pitted concrete with my hands tied over my head, my legs in irons. I received anywhere from 50 to 200 lashes with a fan belt each day, and finally three hours of electric shock torture. I know of at least 20 other prisoners who were similarly tortured over that event, and Ed Atterbury was tortured to death. When Jane Fonda says we weren't tortured, I just don't know what to say— would our scars convince her?"

It is not the purpose here to re-fight the Vietnam War, but, after the US withdrew first its troops and then its economic support in the early Seventies, Communist forces, supported by greatly expanded shipments of military material from the Soviet Union and the People's Republic of China, overwhelmed our erstwhile allies. Since then, literally millions of Cambodians and South Vietnamese have been slaughtered, sent off to "Re-education Camps" never to be heard of again (like the Jews of Europe under Hitler), or thrown ruthlessly into the sea.

The war was long ago, of course, and now most Americans simply want to forget that national pain. Since 1975, when she shared the triumph of the Communist forces that overran Indochina, Fonda has continued her fight against free enterprise as an economic system and in support of centrally-controlled socialism, by whatever name. She is not about to turn her back on her money-making abilities as an actress and said as much at Duke University in 1970: "Members of the political left should take every penny you can get from wealthy liberals. As long as The Movement needs money, I will rip off all I can from Hollywood."

Treason

Treason has been seen by the courts as the most serious offense that can be committed against the United States, a capital offense for which the traditional punishment has been death. Jane Fonda and her allies seem to have convinced the general public that, because Congress did not declare war, it was not possible for her to commit treason when she was in North Vietnam. That is simply not correct. Case law has established the class from which "enemies" can be drawn: "The subject of a foreign power in a state of open hostility with the United States is an "enemy" within this clause defining treason." (Stephen v. United States, 36 F.2nd 87 (1943))

No requirement has ever been specified by the courts for a declaration of war by Congress before treason can be committed. And the Tonkin Gulf Resolution, PL 88-408 (August 1964), gave the President power to "take all necessary steps, including the use of armed force," to assist Southeast Asian allies in defense of their freedom. While not a declaration of war, that is at least formal license granted by Congress for the President to enter into "a state of open hostility", which would require the existence of an "enemy". And an earlier US Supreme Court case held that: "Assembling, joining, or arraying oneself with the forces of the enemy is a sufficient overt act of levying war." (Respublica vs. Carlisle, 1 US 35, 38 (1778))

It would seem that Jane Fonda's posing for pictures in the gunner's seat of an active North Vietnamese anti-aircraft gun that was used to shoot at US aircraft, of which there are ample film records, would constitute a sufficient overt act to have been actually "levying war" against the United States, whether she fired any shots or not. This view is supported by another early Supreme Court decision: "If war be actually levied, all citizens who perform any part, however minute, or however remote from the scene of action, and who are actually leagued in general conspiracy, are considered traitors." (Ex Parte Bollaman, 4 Cranch 75.126 (1807))

Jane Fonda's radio broadcasts from Hanoi would seem to constitute a sufficient overt act for her to be seen as giving aid and comfort to the enemy: "The preparation and making of speeches by defendant in Germany for a broadcast to the United States in order to show discontent with the Government of the United States, to impair the morale of the armed forces and create dissention between the American people and the people of the allied countries constituted treason and the defendant was not protected by the First Amendment guaranteeing freedom of speech." (US vs. Burgman, 87 F. Supp. 568 (1949))

It is a fair appraisal that Jane Fonda may well have committed treason during her visit to North Vietnam, but her present image is such that the probability she will ever be charged and tried as a traitor is almost nonexistent. Sadly, it would seem that sometimes, in this great and glorious land for whose noble principles so many of us offered our lives in Vietnam, the laws just don't apply to famous movie stars like her. However, it is important that all Americans understand the gravity of her actions.

For years I have been accused of being unreasonable on the subject of Jane Fonda's activities. So, for this chapter I thank Tom Carhart and Chuck Allen, who said it better than I could.

There are times when silence is betrayal!

17
Women And Baby Killers

When GIs are called "women and baby killers", I am forced to look at the women in Vietnam and their role in the war.

They played strong roles as attested by Mrs. Nguyen Thi Tu, one of the most powerful in the NLF (National Liberation Front). She was born in Can Tho and raised in Cambodia. A devout Marxist, in 1966 she was named Chairman of the WLA (Woman's Liberation Association). Another woman, Nguyen Thi Dinh, was second in command of the NLF. A general, she was also the deputy military commander of the Army, according to *Pravda* (July 12, 1965).

Women represented half of the population and those over 16 participated strongly in the revolution. Women had to: a) agree to follow the precepts of the association, b) take an active part in the struggle aimed at overthrowing the US Diem clique.

About 1.2 million members worked in the markets, streets, villages; they carried ammunition, ran food to the guerrillas, dug the cross hatch road blocks and fought as guerrillas. Maids to many American GIs, they acted as intelligence agents. Many carved the punji sticks— razor

sharp bamboo sticks covered with excrement. These created untold numbers of casualties.

Families having relatives in the Vietnamese Armed
Forces adhered to Families of Patriotic Soldiers
Association.

Women served to pressure American and South
Vietnamese soldiers to desert, and were part of the NLF
and the Vietnam Mothers Association. They also used
their children to keep watch and to carry messages. The
children used to love to get the GIs repeating after them the
words "Da Dao De Quoc My". Thinking they were counting "one, two, three, four, five", the GIs were really saying, "down with the American Imperialists."

To think that mothers sent their children into the arms of
caring, unsuspecting GIs and watched them blow up together from the explosives attached to the children— My
God!

Women were strongly responsible for the Tet offensive
working. It's interesting to note the role of certain women
in America who were supporting Madame Nguyen Thi
Binh and her long-haired army. Madam Binh, Foreign
Minister and Vice President of the Union of Women for the
liberation of South Vietnam encouraged her American sisters to hold rallies and do all possible to end the war in
Vietnam.

The militia women— regional guerrilla forces, were ex-
pert full-time fighters. In 1965, Ut Tich, who had joined the
guerrillas when she was 14, shot down a helicopter and
killed 35 soldiers.

In the Cu Chi area, women guerrillas destroyed 99 vehi-
cles. Mrs. Ngo Thi May alone killed 25 American soldiers
and three times won the "anti-U.S. Elite Fighter" title. The
Quang Nam women killed 21 Americans and swam the
Bau Nuoc Lon River back home, and returned to their
farming as though nothing ever happened.

The women would gain entrance to US bases, smiling at
the GIs as they paced distances for the nightly mortar
attacks.

It is a small wonder that the GIs came home and had
decent trusting relationships with women at all.

18
Enemies From Within

A director of the Vietnam veterans organization sent me a congratulatory telegram, surprised that President Reagan had recognized Agent Orange. "How did you do it?" he asked. "We've been in Washington lobbying for years and years and couldn't get anything done, and you did it."

While Shad Meshad, with his usual energetic approach, was supporting and congratulating me on the success, a small but angry group of Los Angeles veterans started a hate campaign. They spread rumors, even calling me a traitor and a government agent. In any event, on looking into the group, I learned they were for the most part radicals, leftovers from the Vietnam Veterans Against the War; a few were angry self-admitted communists, and others part of the Center For Veterans' Rights.

Between secret phone calls and indirect hints by other veterans, I began to feel threatened, for the first time in my life, by the very people to whom I was devoting my life. Then I realized that I had lived under other threats when I was in Vietnam. Besides, these threats couldn't have been meaningful as they were coming from just a few who probably needed a scapegoat for their frustrations.

My rationalization did not last long, however. One put a razor to Shad's neck; others threatened to do likewise to me. Suddenly, the Viet Cong were not the only enemies.

I couldn't let them get away with that. Nervous, I went to Los Angeles to face them. I asked to be present at one of their Agent Orange hearings. That day I was late for the hearing. I don't know if it was because I was nervous, or because I was scared. In any event, my being late made things worse. When I got there, I could sense the hostility aimed at me. Some walked by me giving me scornful looks. I just sat there by myself, not saying a word, but jotting down some of the things being said. Mind you, I was being abused and I really did not know or understand exactly what I had done, if anything, against them. In my heart, all I knew was that whatever I had done or was doing could not in any way bring any harm to anyone; the opposite was true as attested by the kind of positive attention and action being directed at the veterans. Scared and nervous, I found the courage to withstand the sneering, the indirect remarks and the coldness. When my time came to speak, in a slightly trembling voice, I began to talk about the effects of Agent Orange—emphasizing that I too had been exposed to it as much, if not more, than some of them in the audience. As I told them about those effects, I began to feel more comfortable with my voice.

"It's not just Agent Orange we have to do something about," I said full-voiced. "The problem starts the minute a veteran walks into a VA hospital in Delayed Stress. The veteran doesn't need a creep to tell him 'There's nothing wrong with you. Take these tranquilizers, go home and get a good night's sleep.'" With that, the audience began to listen; some even smiled while others threw up their arms to show their agreement with what I was saying. "If tranquilizers were all the veteran needed, he wouldn't have gone there in the first place," I added emphatically. "He's there because he's freaking and he doesn't know what's wrong with him. He thinks he's going crazy and he's there for help. What veterans need, when they go for help, is a counselor to say, 'Hey, how you doing? You want to stay here for the night? Come on in, let's talk?' Now, is that too much to ask?" I asked, looking straight into their faces. When a voice from the rear urged me to go on, and feeling a more positive rumbling from the rest, I continued. "That's what the veterans need. Another problem is when a veteran shows up for a 10 o'clock appointment and has to hang around until three in the afternoon to be seen. God forbid if in the meantime he should need to go to the latrine! Should his name be called while in the bathroom, he could lose his place. You see," I pointed out, "we have enemies from within, in the sense that we should do everything possible to make it easier for and on ourselves; instead, those who are paid to help us treat us like animals!" At that, the group became vociferous; their comments stimulated me to go on. "These hospitals belong to us, and we want proper attention and care. Nothing less! My dear brothers, I don't know what it is you have against me. Whatever it is, it is misdirected," I said. At those words, the group exploded with applause. "We have enemies— all of us. And some of these enemies are within. But, don't you worry. We have the where-with-all to win. We've got to stick together and be patient. Too many good things have started going our way. We need to keep it up and work together, united! We're all in this together!"

After that successful meeting, I went to meet Bob Coy from the VA. "Oh, Chris," he said on being introduced, "I know who you are. I've been hearing about you for weeks. I hear Bitzer's calling you a traitor. He wrote in a press release that you were a government agent," he said, pulling from his briefcase a press release from the Center for Veterans' Rights. "'Is it not true that the Veterans Administration sent in a government agent, Chris Noel, to divide the hunger strikers'" he read. At that point, I understood why some veterans had been down on me. They thought I was on the government payroll. I was furious! I didn't get paid to go to Vietnam and I wasn't on anyone's payroll in the veteran's movement.

When one of the veteran leaders learned about my deep disappointment, he took me aside. "Chris," he said, "you can't let this bother you. You have to learn not to let that stuff get to you."

"All right," I blurted, "but it still bothers me."

At a subsequent meeting with another veteran's group, a particular man appearing on a panel discussion made some sly remark about my role and openly laughed, catching the attention of Hank Hahn, then President of Vietnam Veterans of America, which I organized, spending over a thousand dollars to get it started in Southern California. "Chris," he said with empathy, "don't worry about it. We'll straighten it out on another day."

My anger, however, was directed toward Ron Bitzer. When I discovered he may be in one of the wings of the Brentwood VA Hospital, I rushed over. I looked all over the hospital for him, downstairs, upstairs. Unable to locate him, I sat down in an office by the psychiatric complex and began to write him a letter protesting his published reports, and accusing him of trying to discredit me. As I was writing, Shad's kind, devoted and motherly secretary, Betty Jones, told me that she had just seen Ron Bitzer walk by. With the letter in my hand, I rushed out of the office, finally catching up to him by the telephone where he was dialing.

"Ron," I said in an angry voice, "you and I are going to talk." He looked up surprised. Seeing the angry look on my face, he put the receiver down. "Who do you think you are, trying to discredit me, putting out in your press releases that I am a government agent?"

"How did they pay you, Chris?" he asked with a snicker. "How much did they pay you? Did they pay you enough?" he continued with arrogant insistence, convinced that I was *really* a government agent.

"What are you talking about?" I asked, my tone slightly subdued, for I could tell he truly believed in his charges.

"An aide in Morton Blackwell's office told me they paid you to do this."

At that, I got really angry. I was mad, madder than I can ever remember. "Ron," I said after a few moments of pause, "if you'd sit down and talk to me, I can tell you exactly what happened."

"I don't ever want to talk to you. Get out of here; get out of here!" he said angrily. At that, I started to walk away.

"Wait a minute!" I rebounded."How dare you tell me to get out of here. I belong in this VA hospital just as much as you do. You're the one who hates the VA. What're you doing using the VA telephone? Who are you? Let's talk about who you are for a minute, Ron," I challenged him, my dander up. "You're just somebody who lives off the Vietnam veterans. You're just somebody who lives off of our blood and agony, because you weren't even in Vietnam."

"Yeah," he interrupted, "I'm really making a lot of money, aren't I?" he said derisively.

"Somehow or other, you're paying your rent and your bills," I continued angrily. "And if you didn't have this little group how would you pay your bills?"

"Okay, *Miss Delayed Stress*".

In a huff, I headed down the hall, with him behind. "You said you didn't ever want to talk to me, Ron. If you don't want to talk to me, why are you following me? By the way, where were you the day that document came in? I had told you the day before that the White House was calling back. I told you the document was being drawn up and I couldn't find you all day long."

"What about you? You just left. You haven't been around here for the last few months."

"That's right," I blurted, "I went home to Florida."

"I know what they did. They gave you a plane ticket and they gave you money and sent you away so you wouldn't be here for a few months. They paid for you to go away while all this cleared up."

"You know that's not true. Just remember one thing, Ron, I've always earned my living by working hard. I don't appreciate your making up things about me!"

The whole thing was a mess. Even though we kind of cut the edge, we have not really been as friendly as before that incident. What is amazing to me is that there are many veteran leaders from the different veteran organizations who get into these kinds of qualms without realizing how counter productive they are. Certainly, concerning this incident, both Ron and I lost. As for the veterans and the public in general, everyone lost especially because the whole thing was not true, and therefore, unnecessarily harmful. That aide, whoever it is, did his part in creating the split. For what?

I often think about these things. When I read about other similar things in the paper, I think about my own incident, wondering just what the hell is behind it, whether we ever really get the truth.

When I confronted Blackwell, he couldn't believe it. The women in his office said that Ron Bitzer had never called and that if Ron were to call, his calls most likely wouldn't be returned. Maybe, that's what was wrong?

19

My Return

As an actress and spokesperson— it seems I always ended up in New York where I have had some very good times and some very bad ones. In the world of show business, when you're hot, you're hot, and when you're not, you're not.

Back in New York, I stayed with Nikki Haskell, "Miss Big Apple" on 68th Street. As my friend, she took me out every night to parties and discos, and introduced me to many people. I had known her years earlier when we dated the same guy. Now, she has her own cable TV show. With her help, I began to make some important changes in my life, as I wanted very much to be rid of my Delayed Stress. Though I had days when, in spite of my apparent happiness, I had trouble breathing and had several anxiety attacks, I was nevertheless realizing I was having fun in my life and enjoying it thoroughly. I even decided to tune out the Vietnam veterans for the time being—something easier said than done.

I took a job making a commercial for AT&T, and I must admit the money came in handy, for the cost of living in New York is very high.

While waiting for Steve Horn, the director, to call "action", Robert Delbert, an actor, approached me. "Did you do a movie with Steve McQueen?"

"Yes," I answered, surprised. Hardly anyone had ever mentioned having seen me with Steve, though I have so many tremendous memories of him on a personal basis. I even think the movie was good. It had become a favorite cult black and white movie.

"You and I worked together on *Golden Boy* in Herbert Berghoff's acting class," Bob continued. "I kept looking at your teeth, and said to myself, 'I know those front teeth'. I never forget a pair of teeth. You were so bubbly. I was afraid to look into your eyes. The same thing's happening to me now. I'm focusing on your teeth."

To this day, I still don't know what Robert was trying to say. As James Cagney used to say, "Look the other guy in the eye and tell him the truth."

John Wayne

While in Los Angeles I sought all types of medical and therapeutic help. One day, my chiropractor, Dr. Akers, who had been treating my usual nervous disorder, succeeded in making my headaches go away for a while, which meant I could do anything, including eating regular meals.

He told me about some research on Agent Orange in which they found that niacin helped people exposed to paraquat (which is similar to dioxin). The niacin gets into the system and helps break down the poison by getting it out of the body.

Why were the symptoms appearing ten years later? Why were vets getting chloracne, huge sores, nervous spasms and other nervous disorders? I wanted to feel better but sometimes I felt I was getting worse. With time going by, I didn't understand why these things weren't diminishing. It's more than Delayed Stress with me. I honestly felt that I had dioxin in my system because I got sores from time to time. A veteran who happened to see them one day said that I had Agent Orange poisoning.

"What!" I exclaimed.

"Those are Agent Orange sores. I've seen them on other guys."

I wanted to pick at them. But, when I left them alone, the sores went away in a few days.

I stopped taking niacin because I was tired of experimenting on myself. Meanwhile, I was concerned about those vets dying at young ages, dying from cancer.

A Green Beret told me that he was out in the field with John Wayne when a plane sprayed right over them. John Wayne is dead. Two or three of the other guys have also died. Others have cancer. I don't know if this story is true because I don't know his name nor where to find him. That Green Beret just came up to me and said, "You know, there really is such a thing as Agent Orange. I, too, have cancer."

John Wayne was the epitome of a hero in Hollywood war movies. Many GIs said, "Vietnam is not a John Wayne movie." While in Newport Beach in his later years, he said to a friend of mine, "You're looking at a sick man— a very sick man." It's sad to think there's a possibility that "The Nam" might have also killed "The Duke" .

Stress

Stress has been the most popular medical problem and subject for editorial discussions in the early eighties, if not first in these discussions, then next only to Herpes, or AIDS.

The recognition of Post Traumatic Stress Disorder has opened up a Pandora's Box. Lawyers, who specialize in medical cases and who have psychiatrist friends, are loading the courts with cases using PTSD as a behavior pattern that should excuse misdeeds and crimes. Our prison system is no stranger to Vietnam veterans.

According to Dr. Bernard Brown, psychologist, "in addition to its well-known effects on the body, we believe that stress also has an effect on intelligence."

Dr. Brown explained that stress is the major contributor to coronary heart disease, cancer, lung ailments, accidental injuries, cirrhosis of the liver, and suicide. The three best selling drugs are: Tagament for ulcers, Inderal for hypertension, and Valium for anxieties.

"A stressful situation can be good and it can be bad," said Dr. Bruce H. Yaffe. "the difference between good stress and bad stress is if people are in control of it.

"Bad stress leads to anxiety. That is the kind of stress that leads to increased acid production and contractions of the small and large intestine.

"Virtually everybody responds to stress with some form of physical reaction and no part of the body is more vulnerable than the gastrointestinal tract or gut."

According to Dr. Yaffe, large amount of coffee drinking leads to significant acidity. Dr. Yaffe also recommends to stop cigarette smoking and to increase exercises which decreases stress and acid production.

All along, as I continued to have headaches and anxiety attacks, my friend Shad kept saying, "You need more exercise. Train like an athlete— strong body, healthy mind." At first the advice didn't sink in; now finally it has.

Support Systems

Certain population groups enjoy remarkable health and longevity: Mormons, nuns, symphony conductors and women listed in *Who's Who*. This suggests that something in the way these people live, possibly even such abstractions as faith, pride of accomplishment or productivity, may play a role in diminishing the ill effects of stress.

I found that I was lacking a support system of family and friends. I always lived away from home. My many friends around the country were never called on for support— just friendship.

When I started working with the Vietnam veterans, I began to feel the "social support" I needed. Shad was the first to make me realize this. He surrounded himself with terrific people with a common goal of service to humanity. Self-help groups, as I see it now, have replaced the small town hospitality.

Studies of former Vietnam prisoners of war have revealed that communication with fellow captives, sometimes involving complex tapping codes, was a vital factor in their survival. One POW related that even while being beaten by his captors, he could hear other prisoners tapping out the supportive messages— G.B. "God Bless you, Jim Stockdale."

Wayne Newton

At the Veteran's Salute II, which consisted of the unveiling of the GI statue at the Vietnam Veterans Memorial, with President Reagan accepting the entire Memorial on behalf of the American people, I was the Master of Ceremonies for the concert at the Washington Mall. After Frankie Valli performed, I invited the nurses, Gold Star Mothers, and the Red Cross girls on stage. We sang without music *America the Beautiful*. After they left, I told the crowd that "Wayne Newton is still our friend. He is not performing today because the expense money promised by a veteran's group did not come through. It was for travel and band expense. He wanted to be with you."

The crowd started booing. My veteran brothers and sisters, friends and families were booing, obviously expecting him to come anyway. I felt they were booing me instead, and I just wanted to die. "Oh God!" I said to myself, "I can't handle this. I should have kept my mouth shut."

I know what it is to put out a press release informing people of certain things and for those things not to take place.

In the 60's, I had agreed to go to Germany for an Armed Forces Radio anniversary. All I asked for was an airplane ticket. A few days before the event, a wire arrived stating they didn't have the money for the ticket, but I should go there anyway as everyone was expecting me. The problem was that I didn't have the money and did not go. The European papers, however, ran a picture of me with the headline, "Chris Noel is a fink," and further that "She visits the troops in Vietnam but doesn't care about those in Europe." I was so upset. I was condemned even though they didn't live up to their part of the bargain.

In 1965 or 1966, Jack Jones, Steve Lawrence, Eydie Gorme and I had a ringside seat for Wayne Newton's show in Miami. Newton received a standing ovation for his singing. My three friends would not stand up, however. I thought Wayne was super and stood up. Jack reached up and grabbed my arm, pulling on me and telling me to sit down. I was embarrassed and felt they were just jealous of Wayne because he had a standing ovation. They were definitely rude.

Anyway, I felt I should explain why Wayne was not present at the Veteran's Salute II. I'm sure the veterans will understand.

Psychiatric Hospital

While at the New York Agent Orange Victims International, I told Frank McCarthy about my headaches and sleeping problems, and he suggested that I go to the hospital for tests and treatment.

Assured that my Screen Actors Guild Medical Insurance would cover my stay, I packed my clothes and some books and reported to the hospital. When I saw the kind it was, I was shocked. "My friend, Frank, thinks I should be in a psychiatric hospital. I don't believe this. I just don't believe I'm in a psychiatric hospital," I said to myself. When I was told that in New York, state hospitals which do not perform medical operations are called psychiatric hospitals, it didn't do anything to lessen my shock. Even though I had become numb, I signed the papers and sat in disbelief. After a while, a doctor came in and asked why I was there. After telling him about my headaches, he asked me how long I had been depressed.

"How do you know I'm depressed?" I asked, and started to sob. I cried and cried and cried, not able to understand how I had gotten so low as to end up in that place. I hated everybody and didn't want to talk to anyone. When I looked around and saw the other patients, I cried more because I didn't want to be like them or to be one of them.

The next day, Alan Delynn, who was associated with the smash Broadway hit, *42nd Street*, came to see me. I was humiliated and embarrassed because I didn't want him to see me in that condition— no make-up, confused and numb with tears I fought to hold back, to no avail. Besides, as I hadn't told anyone where I was, I don't know how he found out I was there. At that moment, however, I appreciated his visit in spite of my condition.

One day, while on the pay-phone in the hallway, a male patient approached. "You're over three minutes on the phone. You can't use it anymore," he said. How dare that creepy patient tell me I couldn't use the phone! I wanted to hit him.

Another day, my mother called me. "How did you know I was here?" I asked. "I didn't want anyone to know," I said embarrassed. She told me that someone from the hospital had called because the doctors felt I needed a support system and that my parents should know. It never dawned on me to ask my parents for help and support. I always felt I had to handle my life all by myself even though I wasn't doing a good job.

The two-week stay ended up to be three months in the hospital. During that time, I did everything in order to feel better, including giving up marijuana. I didn't have to give up alcohol as I never even liked it.

By not allowing us to stay in our rooms, we were forced to talk to other patients. "I don't think anyone here understands me and I want to say some things to you," I complained during one of our sessions. Given the go-ahead to talk, I rambled on about my life's experiences for over an hour. When I stopped, we were more depressed than before. Slowly, and one at a time, we began to file out and went to our rooms. I had "bummed them out" .

I was anxious, lonely, scared, sad, confused, and disorganized. I expressed fears of contamination by other "sicker" patients, and was more than disturbed on seeing patients go outside the hospital for shock therapy.

So much happened in those three months. I realized that my inability to get decent jobs as a professional actress had gotten to me. Having given up my career in the entertainment world during my marriage, I found it difficult to re-establish myself. With the move to New York, things didn't get better; jobs weren't available to me. I grew more emotionally unstable and teary, and suffered diminished concentration and an acute diminution in self-esteem. At one time, I counted 35 interviews in a row. My agents would send me on commercials castings, but I was not able to book anything, and stopped counting.

Since I knew of PTSD, I had seen a therapist for several months. I stopped after I showed her a picture of me firing a howitzer and expressed my feeling that the thought of it was disturbing me.

"I'm so glad you brought this in," she said. "It proves that you were just a sex object— sending young men off to die and welcoming back the maimed and wounded."

When I told her of my anger to Jane Fonda, she commented, "How can you possibly compare yourself to her? She was born with a silver spoon in her mouth and your anger to her is displaced anger. You use her instead of facing why you really are angry," she said, unable to understand that I felt confused that "Hanoi Jane" could turn on her countrymen and be popular, and I, who supported our soldiers through wholesome entertainment, was so unpopular. It didn't make sense to me.

In 1981, I took the EST (Erhard Seminar Training) in New York. I looked all over for EST at the East Side Terminal. I would do anything to feel better. I was called aside by a trainer who told me that the training there could be very difficult for me. When asked on the enrollment questionnaire if I had seen a psychiatrist, and if so, if I was there with the psychiatrist approval, I said no.

My therapist felt EST to be destructive and I felt her to be destructive. Feeling misunderstood and attacked, I never went back to her, and only wished I hadn't left my picture there.

In the hospital, I lost almost all my wordly possessions, including my condominium in Los Angeles. I asked friends to find buyers to take over the payments, but no one was interested. I also had to sell my 450 SEL Mercedes. Through my friends Thomas Girvin and Richard Castro, I put my furniture and wardrobe in storage. I was out of money. I felt like a complete failure!

I was encouraged to discuss my family as part of the therapy. I saw my real father on and off until the age of twelve. He was an alcoholic, gambler and a womanizer who had been married nine times. He sold used cars and was a bookmaker. I was ashamed of him. The thing that sticks in my mind and kills my heart is the feeling of abandonment. When I told him that, he cried. He never knew.

I disliked him because I did not want to be like him; yet, I saw myself becoming just like him. I certainly looked like him, I thought to myself, during one of my more depressive moods while in my hospital room. Thank God, we became friends when I got to know him before he died. I can now say I loved him, and I am glad we resolved our differences.

In my life, I sought powerful and exciting men who turned out to be alcoholics or otherwise impaired, who have physically and mentally abused me. I never found the soul mate to share my life, a true soul mate who would not misuse and abuse me. I decided, therefore, to stay away from relationships for the time being. All I want is someone to be kind and loving, someone to love and be loved by, who has a sense of humor and has values similar to mine.

Though I'm capable of being self-sufficient, hard-headed and practical, I do want and need protection.

The three months at the hospital went by fast. While there, I celebrated my 41st birthday and realized I was indeed erasing my anger and depression.

Return To My Family

It was very difficult to pack and get all my boxes to the airport for my return home and to have to pay an additional $800 for excess baggage. I just wanted to go home and, thank God, I had the extra money earned while in the hospital. (I was allowed out, with the Doctor's passes, to make a commercial.)

When I got off the plane in West Palm Beach, I was embarrassed to see my nieces and nephews, Mom and Dad. I was the only one in the family to have been in a mental hospital. On seeing me walk as I did, they commented that I looked like a zombie, and I certainly felt like one.

Later I tried jogging, but couldn't do it. I would try running, but had to stop because of dizziness.

I stopped taking my medication, and, for days, I slept with my door open, refusing to be left alone. That fear was so incredible. Loneliness, how terrible, especially when young! Now, at home, one would think things would get better. Instead, I kept being depressed and thinking about my career. I felt like a failure. Furthermore, I did not want the people in my town to know I had been in a mental hospital. The home-town movie star had become a falling star. It took my hometown doctor to discover I had hypoglycemia. I now only eat protein and vegetables.

When the hospital started sending bills, totaling more than $100,000, stating that my insurance did not cover certain costs, I started to have additional nightmares. My stepdad, who had worked two jobs to support us as I was growing up, was still working hard.

My mother, thank God, did all she could to help me through this new emotional crisis. She made my room nice and cheery, with new drapes and bedspreads from the beautiful patterned fabric I had taken from the walls of my Texas home. For the first time, in spite of my problems, I was feeling the comforts I had not known since my childhood. I had great homecooked meals and little hassle. In many ways, I felt secure, secure, secure!

After about two months, I began to feel I was getting better. I even began to feel good when newspapers did stories on me. While on Lee Garen's radio talk show, Bill Treadwell called to encourage me to write this book. As a result, Bill came into my life, and we remained the greatest of friends until his untimely death in February of 1985.

When Patricia Hughes, editor of the *Stars and Stripes*, invited me back to be with the troops at the Vietnam Veterans Memorial Dedication in Washington, I was elated. Questions went through my mind: Would I like the Memorial? Could I handle seeing the veterans? What would I have to do? Do I have the right clothes? Would I be able to handle my anxieties?

My friend Shad encouraged me to accept a part on the entertainment, and I was subsequently happy to be in the company of the fabulous Jimmy Stewart, the master of ceremonies, and of Wayne Newton, the headliner.

Wearing all white, I spoke off stage: "Hi Luv, this is Chris Noel. Remember me?" I asked, the audience responding with thunderous and incredible applause. I was excited, happy and thrilled, and thankful to Patricia Hughes, who had brought me back to my veteran brothers and sisters.

With Martha Raye and Shad Meshad.

With Bruce Springsteen.

Interviewing Don Johnson.

20
The Faith I Never Lost

*A*fter my release from the hospital, I slowly became active in the community, continued with the Vietnam veterans, and picked up with singing, acting in films, as well as doing commercials for television. With the release of my first album, *Forgotten Man*, I was off on a new career.

Florida has always encouraged the arts, and South Florida proved to be a good base for me. I made an industrial film at Epcot-Disney World, commercials, worked with two local bands, and devoted time to the local VVA.

There have been times in my life when I felt I had made bad mistakes. I picked up the same feeling from a lot of veterans who also felt they were wrong. The question is, "Would I do it again?" The answer is, "I most certainly would."

In talking to a friend who was totally against the draft and war, she asked in a very hostile tone, "Would you do it again?" When I gave her my positive answer, she started a tirade against our government and how it had betrayed the American people, etc.

"I don't share your feelings," I blurted, and cut her off. Who needs any more of that bull! There she was, enjoying the fruits of this nation without a sacrifice on her part, and me, with all kinds of problems stemming from taking part in this nation's effort. The gall! The insensitivity! On meeting with these types, I still feel angry.

One of my biggest regrets is realizing I have been too passive with these people, that I should have taken a more definitive position, stood up against people like Jane Fonda. In 1980, for instance, in listening to Jane Fonda's speech in front of about 300 women, I wanted to stand up to challenge her. Instead, I told myself to shut up, even though many of the things she was saying were not true. In the past when I didn't take a stand, I lost respect for myself. I just kept quiet and hung in, just as I did in my marriages. Now I realize that if I want to believe in myself again, I simply must not take a back seat and let things go unchallenged. Perhaps in this new attitude of mine there may be the seed for my survival. It is a matter of survival!

I still remember my feeble challenge to her: "Jane, when you were in North Vietnam, I was in South Vietnam. I don't understand what you are saying here tonight or where you get your information . . . " I said. She answered that she would get back to me to explain about the differences. She never did.

When I started to get involved, Vietnam was already happening, and there was nothing I could do for or against that war. I wasn't judgmental and I didn't condemn anybody. I felt like a doctor having to care for two individuals at the same time, one a GI, the other a VC. I simply chose the GI, much as Hanoi Hannah would have chosen a VC. That Jane may have also chosen a VC is, if it is, a problem for her conscience and that of the American people. My conscience, as harrowed as it may have been, is rather clear and at peace. Whatever pain or joy I may have felt, I did my best.

On several talk shows, including Johnny Carson's, I would always dress in a mini-skirt. In saying that the guys loved legs, the audience laughed. It sounds bizarre; yet, it makes sense. In asking myself, *why*, to some things I do and think, I have even gone to psychics. One of them, a woman, asked, "What were you doing walking among all the blood and guts, and horror?"

To this day, when people learn I was in Vietnam, they invariably ask, "What were you doing there?" And I answer, "Building morale!" What else can I say? Basically, that is what I did. I always felt my purpose was to help others.

Therapy has helped me to raise my self-esteem and get back on my feet.

In February of 1983, I was invited to appear at the VA Medical 50th Anniversary Celebration in Canandaigua, New York. Harry Walters, Administrator of the US Veterans Administration, attended the function. In his formal remarks, he spoke about the controversy over Agent Orange, declaring it the top priority of the Veterans Administration. He said that, "The possible adverse effects of exposure to Agent Orange, ionizing radiation, and other environmental health hazards, continue to be of major concern to veterans, their families, the American public, the Congress, and this Administration. At this time too little is known to answer fully some of these concerns, and this heightened both fear and misunderstanding." I still see the issue ignored, as little is being done.

Ty's Daughter

After reading in the newspapers about my work with POW issues in which I spoke about my tragic marriage to a Vietnam Green Beret, I received an unexpected call from Jamie, Ty's daughter. She and her sister wanted to know about their father and how he really had died. Having been told that he was killed in Vietnam, now, some 15 years later, they were getting a different version. It must have been a shock to them to read that their father had taken his own life.

Needless to say, the call did not help my emotional well being. Nevertheless, I proceeded to tell Jamie about her father, answering all her questions with as many details as possible, my hope was to give these two young women a peace of mind I myself have not had.

More devastating to me was to learn that their mother
(the woman in the silver-framed photograph) was living in
Miami and that she had been working for years at the
Miami Veterans Administration Hospital. I thought she
would have known the value of truth! Ironically, we all live
in South Florida. Maybe Ty did die in Vietnam, and we
didn't know it!

Mother And Child

In San Francisco, while driving with a veteran with
whom I had worked on a documentary project called
"Where Have All The Soldiers Gone?" for which I narrated
and sang the title song— out of nowhere, he started blurt-
ing out about Vietnam, his having been detained in a tiger's cage, etc. Sitting there, listening to him, all of a sudden, whooop! My heart stopped beating: that's what
happens to me each time these veterans tell me their stories. "Oh, no!" I said to myself. "Here we go again. What's
he saying to me? I don't want to hear this. Oh, God! All
right, well, I'm going to be brave and I'm going to sit here
and listen to all this." So, I listened to his story about his
tiger's cage and his eventual escape. I looked at his distraught face and asked, "Have you ever told your wife
about this?"

"No . . . no!"

"Why not?" I asked with controlled empathy.

"Oh, well, I can't. She's a Philippino girl and I can't tell
her about these things."

"Why are you telling me?"

"Well, I know I can talk to you about these things. You
were there. You understand."

"Have you ever told anybody else about this?"

"No!"

With that last *no*, I just let him continue to talk— to let it
out, hopefully to get it out of his system. What he said, of
course, were things I had either directly experienced or
had been told about many times over. When we got to our
destination, I could notice a certain relief on his face. The
confession may have helped him. How about the listener?

That night, I had my recurrent nightmare—bodies and limbs . . .

A couple of months later, he called me. "Listen," I said, "as long as you called me and want to talk to me, even if it's one time a year, I'll tell you exactly how I feel about you. You're running. You've just finished a film about veterans. You know about Post Traumatic Stress Disorder and I'm telling you, you're the classic case of it. You're going to have to stop, take a look at yourself and at what's going on and deal with it.

"I want you to know that I love you very much and I care about you enough as a *Nam* brother that I'm going to be blunt."

He started to cry. When I asked about his wife, he said, "We're divorced. She took the children and went back to the Philippines."

"Did you ever sit down and talk to your wife about your experience in Vietnam?"

"No!", he answered as he had done in the car.

"Have you talked to anybody about them?"

"No, I can't," he answered, his voice muffled.

"Why?" I insisted.

"Because they look at me like they don't believe me. They say, 'Oh, you poor guy.' Or they'll start crying, because they're feeling sorry for me. I don't want people to feel sorry for me."

"What do you want?"

"I just want to be happy."

"Do you ever have any happiness?"

"No, very little."

"What're you going to do about it?" I asked. When he said he was going to get his career together and get his voice tape ready, I stopped him.

"Wait a minute," I said, pushing the telephone close to my mouth so he could better hear me. "You talk about all the externals, all the things you're going to do for your professional life. Those things can't come about when you're so upset inside and you've got to reach over for that bottle of beer or whatever little crutch you've got to reach for. You're not dealing with it. The only way I can tell you these things is because I have to deal with them myself. I realize things happened to me and to my love life and in my career because I also have been confused. Until you have totally dealt with this, you will have inner torment too."

"I'd like to see you. I think you can help me."

"Fine," I answered, and made an appointment.

When he came over a couple of days later, he began to cry. I put my arms around him as he sank his face between my head and shoulder, trying to hide his tears and pains. I brushed my hand over his head. I, who could not have a child of my own—here I was— Mother and Child!

On one of my visits with Shad, in telling him about myself in similar situations as the veteran crying on my shoulder, he explained that I was like a little girl who needed to be guided, who had lost her Mommy and Daddy for a while. I felt that this veteran needed a friend. Remembering that Shad had prescribed a strict regimen of exercises— to get physically strong, make the body strong so the body can beat the head trips— I decided to give the same suggestions to my veteran brother. After calling him on the phone, I went to see him.

In his house, there were two trash baskets filled with beer bottles. I opened the refrigerator for some cold water, and it was full of beer. Without hesitation, I took him to the Vet Center to talk with a counselor. With that arranged, I then drove him to the local beach where he began to feel better. We went for swims, soaked up as much sun as possible, and talked about the various things on his mind. By the end of the day, he looked and acted much better.

Days later, I called the Vet Center and was told that he had not showed up for any of the appointments, having said that he was too busy with work and couldn't break away. I checked a second time, and still, he hadn't shown nor called. "Was it all in vain?" I caught myself asking. It wasn't; it couldn't have been. At the very least, he had one good day of relaxation. And, who knows, some of the things we talked about may have sunk in and be of help to him. Furthermore, he has names and a place he can call or go to, if in need.

Many veterans are not healthy. Emotionally, they are under stress; physically, they are under fear of Agent Orange. If we had only worked together, things would have turned out differently for Vietnam and America. Seeing the faces of Vietnamese and Cambodian refugees, and knowing that hundreds of thousands have been slaughtered, makes me cry with anguish.

Now that it counts, where are the people of "Hell no, we won't go!" Shall we continue to be inconvenienced? Does it mean that we, as the people of this country, will accept only the things that suit us and reject all others? Have we gone through a period of anarchy?

I was never in favor of that terrible war in Vietnam—never! Likewise, I am not in favor of any war. As a citizen of this country— or of any other— I do not have the luxury to choose my wars. Fortunately or unfortunately, government officials do that for us. If only the people of the world would take that right from their elected or appointed leaders! If only the people of the world would have the power to keep tyrants from taking over!

"You were in my ear, on the airways. I never knew if you were in Vietnam, but you were always there," a GI told me.

"I was with you then; I'm with you now. I'm interested in you, not in the war. So, my brothers and sisters, I'll stay with you in our old age. I'll keep learning, fighting and working to improve the quality of our lives. As Brother Joe, who founded the Lord's Place, a hotel for homeless families, said, 'To serve with love is the secret of a happy life.' Well, if that's the secret, then I'm hooked on love. Altruism is wonderful medicine. It allows me to feel good about myself, to reach out to others and lets me forget my own troubles. I now have that sense of purpose so essential to happiness."

What Ever Happened To Miss Christmas?

As time goes by, I find that the more I give to others, the more I get back. The veterans continue to inspire me to go on with my life and to keep working on their behalf.

I am pleased to see that the many veterans groups are getting better organized. Among their latest achievement is the establishment of a computerized national system (CompuServe) through which they can access information on various activities.

Art Fields, a former Green Beret, invited me to sing the *Star Spangled Banner* and *The Ballad of the Green Beret* at the New Orleans Special Forces Association Convention. I felt a sense of calmness and completeness as I was welcomed back into the Green Beret family.

Recently I have gained a new friend, Max Cleland. In no time, he has become my hero. A triple amputee, he was the youngest and first Vietnam veteran in the Senate, and is a former Administrator of the Veterans Administration. In 1984, he was made Secretary of the State of Georgia. Max is one of my daily inspirations. Some veterans feel Max didn't do enough for them. I wonder how much more they want him to bleed.

The way he gets around, takes care of himself, and accomplishes so much, is just amazing. When I get discouraged or depressed, I think of Max's wonderful, strong hugs and strength. Oh, those hugs! (Buscaglia is right!)

I continue to thank the Lord for the strength I've gained from admitting my mistakes. Facing my past and picking myself up has propelled me into an exciting new future.

With jobs becoming more plentiful, I have been working rather steadily, and happy to say that, as a result, I have paid back my debts, especially the medical ones. More importantly, my prayers, the inspiration from individuals, and my undaunted faith, have placed my struggle on another dimension. For me, my struggle is no longer just a matter of survival; it is to live as fully as possible— simply put, to go on with my life, and to give it as much quality as I can muster from within, but without the struggle.

I have time to pursue working with troubled children, noticing the parallel with their problems and the Vietnam veterans: the same resentment, anger, frustration, drug dependency, and wanting to escape. The problems are similar but the roots are different. One is the result of a war, the other the result of innocence induced by that war brought into their homes in living color. The question is, why are there so many similarities? The troubles and anxieties from that era are definitely affecting the children. As I worked with the Palm Beach County Juvenile Services Program, I counsel many kids who are truant and first-time offenders. Since these kids are the children of Vietnam era parents, those who went to war and those who stayed home, I wonder if their anxieties are the products of the same war. I also wonder about the impact of films on the audiences, where they, as the eye of the camera, become the killers, with those horrible scenes of blood, violence, and dismemberment. Those of us who have witnessed these things are not entertained.

I have been concentrating on the advice of famed minister, Dr. Robert Schuller, who said, "Turn your scars into stars." Something good came out of all this: I met Jeff Muldovan, who played a door-gunner in a chopper rescue scene in *Cease Fire*, starring Don Johnson. I played the part of a Vietnam veteran's wife who becomes a widow as a result of his suicide. How ironic! I acted my main scene in one take that brought about unexpected applause from the cast and crew. "Thank you, God, I certainly did not want to repeat the emotional trauma." (One might have commented, "Perfect casting!")

As a result, Jeff wrote the movie script, *Good Morning Vietnam*, which deals with the fictitious rescue of Chris Noel from Cambodian mercenaries by SOG (Special Operations Group).

I have also been creating projects of my own. For example, I created, wrote and developed a script for the TV show, *The New Vets*, aimed at recognizing the achievements of our Vietnam veterans. To help me, I invited vets and the team leader of the Fort Lauderdale Vet Center, to be my co-host. Together we have produced 13 Public Service programs of 30 minutes each, covering a range of subjects from PTSD to Agent Orange.

Having stepped out of our silence, we are now ready to battle injustice and the stigma wrongly attached to us. The phoenix rises: new beginnings, Hope!

In a most wonderful dream, I saw a clear picture of Americans celebrating their heroes and heroines— past and present people who have made America great. That dream has been translated into The Pro America Foundation whose goal is to build *The American Center of Culture and Heritage*, founded by COL K. Hunter and myself. This symbolizes an end and a beginning— the end of an era of pain and divisiveness and the beginning of an era of hope and National unity.

I have always felt that out of human suffering comes a stronger soul. God's wounded often make his very best soldiers.

I have fought the good fight.
I have finished the course.
I have kept the faith.
For the rest,
there is laid upon for me
a crown of justice.

These words were scribbled by an anonymous Marine on a bunker wall in Khe Sanh: "For those who fought for it, Freedom has a flavor the protected will never know."

Epilogue

Soldier

I was that which others did not want to be.
I went where others feared to go,
and did what others failed to do.
I asked nothing from those who gave nothing,
and reluctantly accepted the thought
of eternal loneliness . . . should I fail.
I have seen the face of terror,
felt the stinging cold of fear,
and enjoyed the sweet taste of a moment's love.
I have cried, pained, and hoped . . . but most of all,
I have lived times others would say were best forgotten.
At least someday I will be able to say
that I was proud of what I was . . . a soldier!

"Sky"
George L. Skypeck

Soldier *was generated as a prayer in total exasperation of being an unwelcomed returned disabled Vietnam combat veteran back in America and after an out-of-body experience during which Sky saw friends long since dead in Vietnam. Sky is anticipating that this poem/prayer will be placed on his tombstone someday.*

The Faith I Never Lost.

Index

Answer to Hanoi Han[noi]

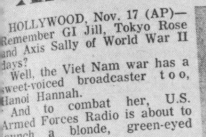

HOLLYWOOD, Nov. 17 (AP)—Remember GI Jill, Tokyo Rose and Axis Sally of World War II days?

Well, the Viet Nam war has a sweet-voiced broadcaster too, Hanoi Hannah.

And to combat her, U.S. Armed Forces Radio is about to launch a blonde, green-eyed weapon of its own.

She's starlet Chris Noel, mini-skirted 5-feet-6 and 115 pounds, with a slightly husky voice and a wide-eyed look that makes her girl next door one moment, woman of the world the next.

"It's going to be a gas," Chris [told an interviewer]. "I'm pick-

hear — but mostly just a feminine home."

Chris is nothing [like the] War II radio sirens [like] Lt. Richard B. [of] Armed Forces Ra[dio]

"Even Hanoi Ha[nnah is the] same. During W[orld War II] you'd get Axis Sa[lly or Tokyo] Rose broadcastin[g to the] GIs.

"But Hanoi Ha[nnah plays the] music the guys l[ike and] throws in a littl[e to make] them homesick.

Chris has spe[nt time] lately touring h[ospitals] wounded GIs fro[m the front]

"But what I [want to do] is go over there [...]

"For now, I [...]

Noel For All Seasons

[Chr]is Noel 'Adopted' by Infantry
[Brin]gs Joy to Troops in Vietnam

[Chris Noel, movie and television star...]

Chris Noel Elevate[s]
Morale In Vietnam

By BOB [...]
HOLLYWOO[D ...]
[...]ring of her [...]
something ou[t ...]
joy of Chri[s ...]

"The Voice"

Starlet Challenge[s]
Hanoi Radio Sire[n]

DATE WITH CHRIS

CHRIS NOEL
THE VIET GIS' ULTIMATE WEA[PON]